THE STUDY OF INTERNATIONAL RELATIONS

INTERNATIONAL RELATIONS INFORMATION GUIDE SERIES

Series Editor: Garold W. Thumm, Professor of Government and Chairman of the Department, Bates College, Lewiston, Maine

Also in this series:

ARMS CONTROL AND MILITARY POLICY—*Edited by Donald F. Bletz**

EASTERN EUROPE—*Edited by Robin Remington**

ECONOMICS AND FOREIGN POLICY—*Edited by Mark A. Amstutz*

THE EUROPEAN COMMUNITY—*Edited by J. Bryan Collester**

INTELLIGENCE, ESPIONAGE, COUNTERESPIONAGE, AND COVERT OPERATIONS—*Edited by Paul W. Blackstock and Frank Schaf, Jr.**

INTERNATIONAL AND REGIONAL POLITICS IN THE MIDDLE EAST AND NORTH AFRICA—*Edited by Ann Schulz*

INTERNATIONAL ORGANIZATIONS—*Edited by Alexine Atherton*

LATIN AMERICA—*Edited by John J. Finan**

THE MULTINATIONAL CORPORATION—*Edited by Helga Hernes*

POLITICAL DEVELOPMENT—*Edited by Arpad von Lazar and Bruce Magid**

SOUTH ASIA—*Edited by Richard J. Kozicki**

SOUTHEAST ASIA—*Edited by Richard Butwell**

SUB-SAHARAN AFRICA—*Edited by W.A.E. Skurnik*

U.S.S.R.—*Edited by David Williams and Karen Williams**

U.S. INVOLVEMENT IN VIETNAM—*Edited by Allan W. Cameron**

*in preparation

The above series is part of the
GALE INFORMATION GUIDE LIBRARY

The Library consists of a number of separate series of guides covering major areas in the social sciences, humanities, and current affairs.

General Editor: Paul Wasserman, Professor and former Dean, School of Library and Information Services, University of Maryland

Managing Editor: Dedria Bryfonski, Gale Research Company

THE STUDY OF INTERNATIONAL RELATIONS

A GUIDE TO INFORMATION SOURCES

Volume 5 in the International Relations Information Guide Series

Robert L. Pfaltzgraff, Jr.

*Director
Institute for Foreign Policy Analysis, Inc.
Cambridge, Massachusetts*

and

*Associate Professor of International Politics
The Fletcher School of Law and Diplomacy
Tufts University
Medford, Massachusetts*

Gale Research Company
Book Tower, Detroit, Michigan 48226

Library of Congress Cataloging in Publication Data

Pfaltzgraff, Robert L
    The study of international relations.

    (International relations information guide series ; v. 5)
(Gale information guide library)
    1. International relations--Bibliography. I. Title.
Z6461.P53   [JX1391]   016.327   73-17511
ISBN 0-8103-1331-6

Copyright © 1977 by
Robert L. Pfaltzgraff, Jr.

No part of this book may be reproduced in any form without permission in writing from the publisher, except by a reviewer who wishes to quote brief passages or entries in connection with a review written for inclusion in a magazine or newspaper. Manufactured in the United States of America.

VITA

Robert L. Pfaltzgraff, Jr., is director of the Institute for Foreign Policy Analysis, Cambridge, Massachusetts. He holds an A.B. degree (1956) from Swarthmore College and M.B.A. (1958), M.A. (1959), and Ph.D. (1964) degrees from the University of Pennsylvania. He is also associate professor of international politics at the Fletcher School of Law and Diplomacy, Tufts University. His primary areas of interest are international relations theory, European regional integration and security, international strategic affairs, arms control, and U.S. foreign policy. He has authored, coauthored, or edited nine books, including CONTENDING THEORIES OF INTERNATIONAL RELATIONS (1971), POLITICS AND THE INTERNATIONAL SYSTEM (2d ed., 1972), SALT: IMPLICATIONS FOR ARMS CONTROL IN THE 1970'S (1973), THE SUPERPOWERS IN A MULTI-NUCLEAR WORLD (1974), CONTRASTING APPROACHES TO STRATEGIC ARMS CONTROL, and THE OTHER ARMS RACE: NEW TECHNOLOGIES AND NON-NUCLEAR CONFLICT (1975) and has published in many periodicals and scholarly journals.

Pfaltzgraff has been the recipient of the Penfield Fellowship (1962-63) and the Guggenheim Fellowship (1968). He has taught at the University of Pennsylvania and served as George C. Marshall Professor at the College of Europe in Bruges, Belgium (1971-72). Between 1973 and 1976 he was director of the Foreign Policy Research Institute, Philadelphia, and editor of ORBIS, a quarterly journal of world affairs. Pfaltzgraff has been a consultant to the Department of Defense, the U.S. Information Agency, and the Department of State. He is a member of the Council on Foreign Relations.

CONTENTS

Preface ix

Chapter 1: The Evolution of the Study of International Relations 1

Chapter 2: Approaches to the Study of International Relations 9

Chapter 3: The Nature of the International System 27

Chapter 4: Foreign Policy and Diplomacy 41

Chapter 5: Power and International Relations 57

Chapter 6: Military Strategy and Theories of Deterrence 67

Chapter 7: Theories of Conflict 85

Chapter 8: Integration and Alliance Theories 101

Chapter 9: Major International Relations Journals 113

Chapter 10: Recommended Books for Small or Personal Libraries 119

Author Index 129

Title Index 135

Subject Index 143

PREFACE

The selected bibliography contained in this volume reflects the theoretical, methodological, and substantive diversity of the contemporary study of international relations. For the most part, the literature annotated in this volume has been published since the Second World War, and the emphasis is on the most recent publications in this field. Books published prior to World War II are included only if they represent a seminal contribution to the literature of international relations or exemplify the evolution of the literature of the field.

Although major journals in the field have been listed, annotations have been restricted to books. Much of the periodical literature has either been reproduced or presented in expanded form in the many anthologies and other books in the field which have appeared in recent years, and which are well represented in this bibliography. Each work is annotated and categorized under the headings most descriptive of its contents, although in many cases writings included in one of the categories of this volume contain some materials appropriate to other categories.

The two chapters that follow the Preface are designed to introduce the reader to the nature and scope of international relations as a discipline and to provide an overview of major approaches to the study of international relations. Chapters 3-8 are devoted to literature on the International System; Foreign Policy and Diplomacy; Power and Theories of Conflict; Military Strategy and Theories of Deterrence; and Integration and Alliance Theories.

In the preparation of this volume I am especially indebted to Jacquelyn K. Davis, of the Institute for Foreign Policy Analysis, Cambridge, Massachusetts, for assistance in the selection and annotation of entries and in the preparation of introductions to the literature in each of the sections into which the volume is divided. Judy Crosby and Joanne Gowa, formerly of the Foreign Policy Research Institute, as well as Robert Helm, while a student at the Fletcher School of Law and Diplomacy, Tufts University, assisted. Last but not least, Kathryn B. Wainwright provided invaluable help in the typing of the manuscript.

Chapter 1

THE EVOLUTION OF THE STUDY OF INTERNATIONAL RELATIONS

International relations is relatively new as an autonomous field of study. Although international relations courses were not offered in American colleges and universities until after World War I, the intellectual roots of the field lie deep in the past. The problems of power and its management--a concept central to the writings of many scholars throughout history--were of concern to writers such as Thucydides, Machiavelli, and Clausewitz. The study of international law was of interest to scholars of the early modern period, and a burgeoning literature of international law developed as early as the sixteenth century. Historians had as a major concern the study of diplomatic relationships among nations long before the emergence of international relations as an autonomous field of study.

Classical and contemporary scholars have defined international relations as a field of study having as its broad purpose the analysis and understanding of relations among the major groups into which the world is divided, especially those capable of acting independently of each other. Although its primary focus has been interactions among nation-states, the scope of international relations embraces the study of the nature and structure of international systems, past and present, and actual and hypothetical, as well as nonstate actors such as multinational corporations and transnational actors like the Organization of Petroleum Exporting Countries (OPEC).

Scholars have long attempted to understand and explain such phenomena as conflict among peoples and the conditions necessary for fostering greater cooperation and political integration, as well as the impact of politics and political structures on foreign policies and international-domestic linkages. Over the past generation, increasing numbers of scholars have focused attention on such topics as the structure of the international system; foreign policy decision-making processes, with emphasis on the study of personality and bureaucratic motivation factors; the comparison of foreign policies; patterns of interaction within decisional units; and communications among decision makers. In addition, there have been major efforts to study decision making during international crises; to develop theories of conflict and of political integration; and to evolve theories of deterrence and escalation. The advent of nuclear weapons gave rise to strategic or international security studies in American universities and, in a broader academic research community concerned with policy research, greater interest in conflict analysis and the development of theories of deterrence and arms control. A variety of other disciplines, including history, political science, economics, psychology, sociology, and anthropology, have contributed to these and other studies of international relations. As a result, the contemporary study of international relations is characterized by numerous concepts, theories, approaches, and methodologies.

Whereas scholars have long studied international law in terms of the state and sovereignty and the nature of power and its management, international relations, in its formative period in the aftermath of World War I, was addressed largely to the study and understanding of the causes of conflict for the purpose of building a more peaceful world.[1] In its early years, however, the study of international relations, as observed by E.H. Carr, was at the "initial stage in which little attempt is made at critical analysis of existing facts or available means."[2] Rather than focusing principally on analyses of the behavior of the actors in the international system, the early international relations literature was devoted largely to the study of international law and organization and to the development of proposals for a more peaceful world.

Thus international relations studies often were addressed to normative analyses--that is, the study of what <u>ought</u> to be, rather than the systematic examination of the world as it was. In fact, one of the unresolved debates among scholars is the extent to which international relations should focus on value-free studies as opposed to normative and policy-oriented analysis. Normative, or utopian, theories of international relations generally condemned national behavior based on pursuit of power politics to satisfy national interests and, instead, urged states to act according to the higher standards established by international law and organization. According to the premises underlying utopian theory--derived intellectually from the eighteenth century Enlightenment--man is good or, at any rate, capable of improvement through education and changes in his environment. At the international level, political behavior, it was postulated, could be altered so that man would foresake power politics in favor of a collective security system based on the League of Nations.

The events of the 1930s eroded the assumptions and premises of utopian thought. The gap between utopian theory and political practice widened as the Japanese invaded Manchuria, Mussolini occupied Ethiopia, and Hitler violated, again and again, the provisions of the Treaty of Versailles and embarked upon his conquest

---

[1] E.H. Carr, THE TWENTY YEARS' CRISIS 1919-1939: AN INTRODUCTION TO THE STUDY OF INTERNATIONAL RELATIONS (No. 8) details the emergence of the discipline of international relations, emphasizing its intellectual origins and the assumptions underlying the differing approaches. See also Nos. 4, 13, 20, 27, 45, and 64.

[2] Ibid., p. 8.

of Europe. Against this foreboding international environment, international relations scholars were endeavoring to develop other approaches to the study of international relations. In Britain, Lewis F. Richardson completed a pioneering study on the relationship between arms races and wars, using mathematical models and statistical analyses.[3] The quantitatively-oriented scholars of a more recent generation are indebted intellectually to Richardson's analysis based on the use of statistics in conflict studies. In the United States, Quincy Wright produced a monumental survey and comparison of wars in an effort to develop a comprehensive theory of conflict.[4] Wright's writings provided a basis for much of the research of a later generation. Other scholars writing in the 1930s and 1940s, such as Harold Lasswell, initiated international relations research on the relationship between world politics and personality factors;[5] others, such as Hans Kohn, Ellsworth Huntington, Nicholas Spykman, and Robert Strausz-Hupé, explored the effects of nationalism, geography and geopolitics, climate, population, and migration on international relations.[6] Thus, by the 1940s the study of international relations reflected the interest of scholars in the analysis of major forces and actors shaping world politics, as well as the systematic study of the nature and causes of conflict.

The dominant school of thought, however, was the so-called realist theory, which purported to describe interstate behavior and to provide a framework for the analysis of foreign policy. In many ways, utopian and realist theories represent contrasting approaches to the study of international relations. In contrast to the normative emphasis of utopianism, realist scholars sought to study the world as they perceived it to be. In utopianism, politics was seen as a function of ethics; to the realist, ethics became a function of politics. According to Hans J. Morgenthau, the realist sought "to reduce the fact of experience to more specific instances of general propositions."[7] Realist scholars such as Hans J.

---

[3] Lewis F. Richardson, ARMS AND INSECURITY (No. 312) and STATISTICS OF DEADLY QUARRELS (No. 313).

[4] Quincy Wright, A STUDY OF WAR (No. 327).

[5] Harold Lasswell, WORLD POLITICS AND PERSONAL INSECURITY (No. 301).

[6] See, for example, Ellsworth Huntington, CIVILIZATION AND CLIMATE (No. 90); Robert Strausz-Hupé, GEOPOLITICS: THE STRUGGLE FOR SPACE AND POWER (No. 204); Hans Kohn, THE IDEA OF NATIONALISM: A STUDY OF ITS ORIGINS AND BACKGROUND (No. 97); and, Nicholas Spykman, AMERICA'S ROLE IN WORLD POLITICS: THE UNITED STATES AND THE BALANCE OF POWER (No. 201).

[7] Hans J. Morgenthaus, POLITICS AMONG NATIONS (No. 106), p. 27. See also Nos. 8, 13, 27, 41, and 64.

Morgenthau and George F. Kennan[8] identify power and its pursuit to be the explanatory variable underlying all, or most, international behavior. According to Morgenthau, "International Politics, like all Politics, is a struggle for power."[9] Nations pursue interests through the development and use of power and their foreign policies represent a continuing effort to maintain and increase power by attempting to check or reduce the power of other nations. The absence of definable authority based on effective sanctions in the international community imposes upon the state a morality that differs radically from that which governs man as an individual within society. Thus, realist theory mirrors Machiavelli's conception that "the state creates morality as well as law and that there is neither morality nor law outside the state."[10]

International relations scholars--above all, members of the realist school--have long been interested in the problem of power and its management. No approach has generated as much interest, discussion, and controversy as has that of balance of power. As Ernst Haas observes: "A very large number of writers since the Renaissance . . . have concerned themselves with perfecting overall theories of international relations on the basis of the balance of power."[11] In utopian theory, collective security was developed as an alternative to balance of power, since the formation of alliances within a European balance of power had allegedly contributed to the outbreak of World War I. In turn, the failure of collective security in the League of Nations contributed to the rise of realism, with its emphasis on the balance of power, as a dominant school of thought in the United States. If utopianism contained, as noted earlier, the assumption that man is inherently good, or at least improvable, the realist conception viewed man as evil, power seeking, and not capable of effecting basic change in his nature.

The balance of power concept accorded with realist thought because it eschewed schemes dependent for their success on major changes in man or his environment, but sought instead to balance man against man, nation against nation, evil against evil. Of those who have studied the balance of power, none is more widely identified with it today, both as a scholar and policymaker, than Henry A. Kissinger.[12] According to balance of power theory, peace and sta-

---

[8]George F. Kennan, REALITIES OF AMERICAN FOREIGN POLICY (New York: W.W. Norton, 1966).

[9]Morgenthau, POLITICS AMONG NATIONS (No. 106), p. 27.

[10]Hans J. Morgenthau, IN DEFENSE OF NATIONAL INTEREST (No. 150), p. 34.

[11]Ernst Haas, "The Balance of Power, Prescription, Concept, or Propanganda," WORLD POLITICS 5 (July 1953): 443-44. See also Nos. 8, 13, 18, 55, 67, and 68.

[12]Henry A. Kissinger, A WORLD RESTORED: THE POLITICS OF CONSERVATISM IN A REVOLUTIONARY AGE (No. 95).

bility are attained by an equilibrium of forces among nations and among alliance systems. Central to balance of power is the notion of legitimacy, defined as "international agreement about the nature of a workable arrangement and about the permissible methods and aims of foreign policy."[13] Thus, under conditions of a balance of power, a diplomacy and statecraft characterized by maneuver assume great importance in the pursuit of foreign policy objectives.

Realist theory has contributed both to the policy relevance of international relations and to the development of new conceptual frameworks for studying international phenomena. At the same time, realist writers have been criticized for allegedly being excessively preoccupied with power as a central concept. In addition, there has been concern about the lack of precision in realist writings in defining concepts such as power, national interest, and balance of power, and the difficulty of subjecting such concepts to rigorous measurement and analysis. Although more traditional scholars of international relations insisted that their methods were meticulous, logical, and precise, a new generation of scholars sought to develop alternative approaches to the study of international relations, based on the use of quantification to validate hypotheses and to contribute to international relations theory.

By the 1960s much of the study of international relations had shifted toward the development of greater conceptual precision and the building of empirically-based theories. Drawing upon the literature of the philosophy of science, scholars addressed themselves to questions about the nature and purpose of theory and the techniques appropriate to the validation of theory in international relations. Discussion abounded about definition and scope, as well as the extent to which international relations existed, or should exist, as an independent, or autonomous, discipline, or field of study. Efforts were made to define more clearly the basic units of international relations; to delineate and distinguish among the international system, the states as actors, and the individual as discrete levels of analysis, and to make use of concepts and methods drawn from other disciplines. Systems theory, field theory, cybernetics, decision-making theory, role theory, game theory—to mention but a few—are illustrative of concepts borrowed from other disciplines such as sociology, economics, mathematics, and psychology. Proponents of the behavioral study of international relations, utilizing methods based on content analysis, survey research, simulation, and statistics, contended that much of the international phenomena under observation could be quantified and that patterns of similarity among various and seemingly diverse events could be discerned. Emphasis, therefore, was placed on the development of greater conceptual precision, and on the formulation and testing of hypotheses and the construction of models or theories based upon logically interlinked hypotheses. While the traditionalist was usually, but not always, concerned with single-case analysis, the quantitatively-oriented scholar focused on the analysis of recurring patterns among many instances of the political behavior under study, about which generalizations are

---

[13]Ibid., p. 2.

subsequently made. While earlier generations of scholars had studied history as a succession of unique events, the behavioralist sought to utilize history more systematically in order to determine recurring patterns.

The behavioralist-traditionalist controversy, like the realist-utopian debate, led to a divergence among scholars about the study of international relations that has yet to be fully resolved. According to one critic of behavioralism, Hedley Bull, the behavioralist is allegedly too confident of his ability to make generalizations and to convert an ambiguous probability into causality and to use it for making predictions in a sphere that is not predictable.[14] The behavioralist is criticized for attributing to abstract models a congruence with reality that they do not have or for employing abstractions that are detached from reality; for avoiding the substantive issues of international politics because in his zeal for scientific method he has never really mastered those issues in all their complexity; and for succumbing to a "fetish for measurement" that ignores crucially important qualitative differences among the things being measured.

In contrast, the behavioralist asserted that, for example, in testing for statistical correlation between two factors, he was trying to determine whether the relationship between them might have been merely coincidental, and when he engaged in multivariate analysis he was attempting to discover which of several factors constitutes the most reliable predictor of a particular outcome.[15] The scientific analyst regarded the traditionalist's distrust of precise methods, quantification and verification through statistical testing, as misconceived.[16] The traditionalist retorted that, in his own way, he performed a careful "content analysis" of the primary and secondary sources (documentary and otherwise) which he adduced as evidence--speeches, press statements, government reports, diplomatic messages, personal memoirs, newspaper accounts and commentaries, interviews, and scholarly studies--and intuitively selected the important and relevant without the precise systematic counting of words and phrases. The traditionalist remained convinced that the essence of politics is the qualitative differences--that subtle shade or nuance of meaning communicated in the choice of a single word or phrase but does not lend itself to quantification. To the charge that the scientist glossed over relevant differences between the phenomena being counted, one leading spokesman of the scientific school rejoined as follows:

---

[14] The article by Hedley Bull, together with a series of essays dealing with the traditionalist-behavioralist controversy, is found in Klaus Knorr and James N. Rosenau, eds., CONTENDING APPROACHES TO INTERNATIONAL POLITICS (No. 32), pp. 20-38. See also Nos. 13, 16, 23, 29, 30, 32, 33, 42, 53, and 54.

[15] J. David Singer, "The Incompleat Theorists: Insight Without Evidence," (Knorr and Rosenau, CONTENDING APPROACHES (No. 32), pp. 72-73.

[16] Knorr and Rosenau, "Tradition and Science in the Study of International Politics," in CONTENDING APPROACHES, (No. 32), p. 16.

Evolution of International Relations

> In due course the various measurement efforts will show us where we have erred in lumping the unlumpable. But it seems to me that this undue preoccupation, yea obsession, with the unique, the discrete, the noncomparable, is what has largely kept history from developing into a cumulative discipline and has led to so much frivolous debate between the quantifiers and the antiquantifiers. . . . The fact is that no two events, conditions or relationships are ever exactly alike; they must always differ in location. The question is whether they are sufficiently similar to permit comparison and combination for the theoretical purposes at hand. To borrow a metaphor of which the antiquantifiers are fond, there is absolutely nothing wrong with adding apples and oranges if fruit is the subject at hand![17]

While the trend in the study of international relations, not dissimilar to that in the study of other social sciences, has evolved toward greater emphasis on quantification, there is growing recognition of the compatibility between quantitative and qualitative approaches in a "post-behavioral phase" of international relations. Reviewing the behavioral phase and recognizing the need for greater synthesis between qualitative and quantitative approaches, James N. Rosenau, an early proponent of the behavioral school, especially in the study of foreign policy, asks:

> . . . . Where are the models that command attention? What theories are widely endorsed? What findings have been established? What do we know about the dynamics of international life that is new and important? Could it be that our methodological progress has led us nowhere? Are we stressing the need for new teaching methods because we lack new substantive materials to teach? Have we become so preoccupied with improving our ties to the policy-making community because our research interests are no longer self-sustaining? Is assessing ourselves a substitute for assessing substantive problems?[18]

While continuing to strive for a synthesis among the older and newer approaches to the study of international relations, and to develop new methods of research and to derive generalizations about diverse phenomena, there has been greater recognition in the 1970s of the need to link more systematically theories of international relations to public policy. As Rosenau points out, the graduate training in statistical, mathematical, and data analysis methods seems to have been excessively concerned with technical problems to the relative neglect of

---

[17]Singer, in Knorr and Rosenau, CONTENDING APPROACHES, (No. 32), p. 77.

[18]James N. Rosenau, "Assessment in International Studies," INTERNATIONAL STUDIES QUARTERLY, June 1975, p. 340.

the substantive problems to which the methods may be applied.[19] The post-behavioral phase includes an increasing emphasis, once again, on normative aspects of international relations. Behavioralism has been criticized for its allegedly excessive preoccupation with methodology and under-emphasis on ethical considerations. While the world faces formidable, and perhaps insurmountable, problems resulting from technology--resource and food shortages, unprecedented destructive capabilities, environmental challenges, and population growth--the focus of international relations, according to some behavioral critics, has been on problems chosen by virtue of available methodologies. Concern with shaping the evolving future has led to a greater interest in futurology and technological forecasting, as well as the development of models of alternative future worlds, together with policy recommendations for moving from the flawed present to an allegedly less dangerous future.

In the period ahead, the study of international relations is likely to emphasize, to a greater extent than in the recent past, the development of links between theory and practice. In this regard, scholars can be expected to maintain their quest for more accurate and reliable theories of conflict, integration, and decision making, to mention a few areas of concern in the study of international relations. But the development of conceptual and methodological tools to anticipate change will increase in importance. The quickening transformation in the international system resulting from the pervasive impact of science and technology on peoples around the world, the growing penetrability of societies to influences from outside their boundaries, the inadequacy of institutions and practices inherited from the past in enabling man to cope with the global issues of the last quarter of the twentieth century, will challenge the theorist and practitioner, the scholar and policymaker.

In the various theory-building efforts of the future, it will be essential to achieve a greater balance and a synthesis between empirical-analytic theory and normative theory, and between basic and applied research. Although the gap between quantitative and qualitative approaches and their respective proponents remains great, many of the existing approaches and methods are, or can be made, mutually reinforcing. Normative theory can suggest alternative goals and preferences for political leaders, as well as propositions for systematic research, and theory based on quantitative analysis can furnish guidance as to the kinds of policy choices essential for the achievement of desired goals. Although such a synthesis has not emerged in the literature of international relations, it represents an important prerequisite to the creation of approaches, theories, and methodologies relevant to the needs of the policymaker. The annotated bibliography in this volume is illustrative not only of the evolution of the study of international relations, but also of the significant gaps in substance as well as in methodology and theory; and thus demonstrates the present achievements, future prospects, and inherent limitations of international relations literature.

---

[19] Ibid., p. 345.

Chapter 2
APPROACHES TO THE STUDY OF INTERNATIONAL RELATIONS

1 Banks, Arthur S., ed. POLITICAL HANDBOOK OF THE WORLD 1975. New York: McGraw-Hill Book Co., 1975. 512 p.

   The most recent edition of a highly useful reference volume published annually since 1927 by the Council on Foreign Relations, this handbook contains basic information on the political systems, history, geography, population, and economies of 160 nations. Included are facts on political leaders as well as alliances and international organizations.

2 Bobrow, Davis B. INTERNATIONAL RELATIONS: NEW APPROACHES. New York: Free Press, 1972. 95 p.

   An introductory analysis of recent analytic frameworks for the study of such phenomena as decision making; conflict; perception and escalation; the spread of nuclear weapons; conditions for political stability; international systems; and political gaming. The author examines the nature of quantification and compares and contrasts the newer and older approaches to the study of international relations.

3 Bobrow, Davis B., and Schwartz, Judah L., eds. COMPUTERS AND THE POLICY-MAKING COMMUNITY: APPLICATIONS TO INTERNATIONAL RELATIONS. Englewood Cliffs, N.J.: Prentice-Hall, 1968. 374 p.

   A volume containing sixteen writings on such topics as the logic of computers; computer languages; information retrieval; content analysis in political research; the use of computers in simulations and war games; survey research; and problems of designing a computer simulation of international relations.

4 Buell, Raymond Leslie. INTERNATIONAL RELATIONS. New York: Henry Holt and Co., 1925. 768 p.

   An early textbook designed to survey international relations as a field of study distinct from international law. The volume contains an analysis of problems of nationalism and internationalism; the causes and nature of imperialism and national self-determination; the settlement of international disputes; and international organization.

5   Burton, J.W. INTERNATIONAL RELATIONS: A GENERAL THEORY, Cambridge: Cambridge University Press, 1965. 288 p.

The author develops a framework for the study of international relations based on decision-making and communications theories. Changes in the international environment--nuclear weapons, new states, international organization, increasing levels of interaction--allegedly render traditional theories inadequate and make necessary new models to describe contemporary international relations.

6   _____. SYSTEMS, STATES, DIPLOMACY AND RULES. New York: Cambridge University Press, 1968. 251 p.

A systems approach to the study of international relations in which the author relates contemporary international relations theory to the practice of diplomacy and the resolution and avoidance of conflict. Included are analyses of decision making; the role of state power; crisis behavior; problems of multinational and divided states; intervention; and international organization in a world of nation-states.

7   _____. WORLD SOCIETY. New York: Cambridge University Press, 1972. 180 p.

A concise, basic text designed to present an interdisciplinary approach to the study of international relations. Included are analyses of behavioral science and the postbehavioral revolution; conceptualizing and models; the nature of conflict and its resolution; values; and the idea of national interest and nationality in decision making.

8   Carr, E.H. THE TWENTY-YEARS' CRISIS, 1919-1939: AN INTRODUCTION TO THE STUDY OF INTERNATIONAL RELATIONS. New York: St. Martin's Press; London: Macmillan, 1939. Reprint. New York: St. Martin's Press, 1962. 244 p.

A lucid, trenchant, and important contribution to the literature of international relations theory. The author traces the intellectual antecedents of utopian and realist approaches, and presents an analysis and critique of utopianism and realism in the interwar study of international relations. Included are examinations of the foundations of international law, the nature of power, and the relationship between utopianism and realism in promoting peaceful change and enhancing the prospects for a new international order.

9   Coplin, William D. INTRODUCTION TO INTERNATIONAL POLITICS: A THEORETICAL OVERVIEW. 2d ed. Chicago: Rand McNally College Publishing Co., 1974. 460 p.

   An overview of the major concepts and propositions utilized in the study of international politics, this work is focused on the behavior of states and developing categories for comparative foreign policy analysis. The author draws upon concepts from the fields of organizational behavior, political culture and socialization, bargaining, and game theory for the analysis of contemporary international politics. In addition to war-peace issues, the broader environment in which international politics takes place is considered. Each chapter contains a bibliographic essay containing additional literature.

10 _____, ed. SIMULATION IN THE STUDY OF POLITICS. Chicago: Markham Publishing Co., 1968. 365 p.

   A collection of twelve writings on the use of simulation in the study of international politics and in other fields of political science, including urban affairs, organizational behavior, elections, and political development. Among the topics examined are decision makers' environments in the Inter-Nation Simulation, the assumptions of international relations simulations, and the propositions from international relations theory utilized in simulation.

11 Coplin, William D., and Kegley, Charles W., Jr., eds. ANALYZING INTERNATIONAL RELATIONS: A MULTIMETHOD INTRODUCTION. New York: Frederick A. Praeger, 1975. 381 p.

   An introductory anthology designed to provide both a substantive and methodological overview of international relations as a field of study. Included are selections on quantitative, psychological, and bureaucratic approaches to the analysis of foreign policy; models of international systems; international law; conflict escalation and reduction; and political integration and intergovernmental organization.

12 Deutsch, Karl W. THE ANALYSIS OF INTERNATIONAL RELATIONS. Englewood Cliffs, N.J.: Prentice-Hall, 1968. 214 p.

   Synthesizing and building on earlier work on international integration and transaction flows and systems theory, the author sets forth a framework for the study of contemporary international relations. Included are analyses of the nature and causes of conflict; assessments of groups, interests, and elites in the foreign policy process; the role of diplomacy, alliances and coalitions; a critique of theories of deterrence and escala-

Approaches to International Relations

tion; and the prospects for regional and global organizations in promoting international integration.

13 Dougherty, James E., and Pfaltzgraff, Robert L., Jr. CONTENDING THEORIES OF INTERNATIONAL RELATIONS. Philadelphia: J.B. Lippincott Co., 1971. 416 p.

An overview, synthesis, and analysis of major theoretical approaches to international relations. Included are analyses of early approaches to international relations theory; the balance of power; the nature of scientific theory; man-milieu relationships; political realism; systemic theories; economic theories of imperialism and war; microcosmic and macrocosmic theories of conflict; theories of nuclear deterrence and arms control; theories of international integration, regionalism and alliance cohesion; decision-making theories; game theory, bargaining, and gaming; and international studies in the 1970s. The volume contains extensive bibliographical references to the literature, older and contemporary, of international relations theory.

14 Duchacek, Ivo D. NATIONS AND MEN: AN INTRODUCTION TO INTERNATIONAL POLITICS. Hinsdale, Ill.: Dryden Press, 1975. 596 p.

An introductory textbook designed to analyze existing patterns of international interaction, rather than to present proposals for the restructuring of global relationships. The author emphasizes the role of ideologies, perceptions, and perceptual distortions at the individual and group levels, and examines the territorial dimension of international politics; nationalism; foreign policy decision making; international law and organization; deterrence; international power balances in the nuclear age; and collective security and diplomacy.

15 Farrell, John C., and Smith, Asa P., eds. THEORY AND REALITY IN INTERNATIONAL RELATIONS. New York: Columbia University Press, 1967. 108 p.

An anthology containing seven writings on such topics as the nature of theory in international relations, international structure, national force, and the balance of power; the notion of sovereignty; the Lockean tradition in American foreign policy; and normative theory in international relations.

16 Farrell, R. Barry, ed. APPROACHES TO COMPARATIVE AND INTERNATIONAL POLITICS. Evanston: Northwestern University Press, 1966. 368 p.

An anthology containing twelve writings illustrative of a variety of qualitative and quantitative approaches to the study of politics, with special emphasis on the development of a more comparative analysis of foreign policy. Included are essays on such topics as external influences on the internal policies of states; the nature of foreign policy, respectively, in developed and developing countries; foreign policy in "open" and "closed" systems; and comparisons between international and intranational politics.

17 Finlay, David J., and Hovet, Thomas, Jr. 7304: INTERNATIONAL RELATIONS ON THE PLANET EARTH. New York: Harper and Row, 1975. 374 p.

A highly normative analysis of the global future based on a critique of traditional conceptions of national interest; isolationism; conflict; and competition, together with the authors' prescriptions for resolving the issues discussed in this volume, which is intended primarily for undergraduate use. Included are chapters on contending descriptions, models, and theories of the international system; decision making; environmental forces; economic development; the use of force; diplomacy; and alliances.

18 Forsyth, M.G., et al., eds. THE THEORY OF INTERNATIONAL RELATIONS: SELECTED TEXTS FROM GENTILE TO TREITSCHKE. New York: Atherton Press, 1970. 353 p.

A selection of writings dealing with the nature of interstate relations, the causes of war, the balance of power, laws of war and peace, the nature of the state, and the idea of federations or confederations of states by leading scholars of international law and Western political theory.

19 Forward, Nigel. THE FIELD OF NATIONS: AN ACCOUNT OF SOME NEW APPROACHES TO INTERNATIONAL RELATIONS. London: Macmillan Co., 1971. 207 p.

A review and critique of selected American behavioral approaches and "mini-theories" of international relations by a British scholar. Focusing on game theory, simulation, and communication models, the author assesses the potential, as well as the limitations of quantitative approaches to international relations.

20 Fox, William T.R. THE AMERICAN STUDY OF INTERNATIONAL RELATIONS. Columbia: University of South Carolina Press, 1968. 116 p.

A selection of the author's published writings on international relations research between the two world wars, the teaching of international relations in the United States, the contribution of Frederick Sherwood Dunn to the American study of international relations, the uses of theory, and the evolution of international relations as a field of study.

Approaches to International Relations

21   _____, ed. THEORETICAL ASPECTS OF INTERNATIONAL RELATIONS. Notre Dame, Ind.: University of Notre Dame Press, 1959. 118 p.

     A series of essays on the nature, limits, and uses of international relations theory, the actors in international politics, and the meaning of power and ideology in national and international affairs.

22   Guetzkow, Harold, et al. SIMULATION IN INTERNATIONAL RELATIONS: DEVELOPMENTS FOR RESEARCH AND TEACHING. Englewood Cliffs, N.J.: Prentice-Hall, 1963. 248 p.

     A description of a man-computer model for the simulation of international relations. In a volume written in the early stages of the internation simulation project, the contributors discuss the use of simulation in the study and teaching of international relations, provide information about the evolution of the internation simulation project, and report on the results of simulation exercises completed in the early 1960s.

23   Haas, Michael, ed. INTERNATIONAL SYSTEMS: A BEHAVIORAL APPROACH. New York: Chandler Publishing Co., 1974. 433 p.

     A textbook in which eight contributors survey the major theories, methodologies, and research findings that have emerged from the behavioral study of international relations. Included are chapters on such topics as the scope and method of international relations; international socialization; nonalignment; integration; decision making; deterrence; and conflict resolution.

24   Harrison, Horace V., ed. THE ROLE OF THEORY IN INTERNATIONAL RELATIONS. Princeton, N.J.: D. Van Nostrand Co., 1964. 118 p.

     A collection of five original essays whose authors probe substantive and methodological problems of theory building. Included are analyses of the nature of a general theory of international relations; the origins and uses of theory; and the intellectual and political functions of a theory of international relations.

25   Hartmann, Frederick H. THE RELATIONS OF NATIONS. 4th ed. New York: Macmillan Co., 1973. 715 p.

     An introductory text in which the author sets forth a three-level theory based on the individual, the state, and the international system. Included are analyses of sovereignty and nationalism; national power; conflict and its resolution; arms control and disarmament; the balance of power; diplomacy; and the foreign policies of major powers.

Approaches to International Relations

26   Hermann, Charles F., ed. INTERNATIONAL CRISES: INSIGHTS FROM BEHAVIORAL RESEARCH. New York: Free Press, 1972. 334 p.

> An important volume containing essays on recent quantitative research on international crises. Included are chapters based on comparative case studies; studies of perceptions of crises by policymakers; political gaming and crisis behavior; crisis bargaining and management; and alternative models of international crisis.

27   Herz, John H. POLITICAL REALISM AND POLITICAL IDEALISM. Chicago: University of Chicago Press, 1951. 275 p.

> An important analysis of theories of idealism and realism and their intellectual antecedents in the study of international relations. Included are an examination of the nature of power and an assessment of the utility and limitations of idealism and realism as essential ingredients of an adequate foreign policy.

28   Hoffmann, Stanley. THE STATE OF WAR: ESSAYS IN THE THEORY AND PRACTICE OF INTERNATIONAL POLITICS. New York: Frederick A. Praeger, 1965. 276 p.

> A collection of essays originally published elsewhere. Included are the author's analyses of the nature of theory and international relations; Rousseau on war and peace; international systems and international law; restraints and choices in American foreign policy; terror in theory and practice; and distinctions between domestic politics and foreign policy.

29   _____, ed. CONTEMPORARY THEORY IN INTERNATIONAL RELATIONS. Englewood Cliffs, N.J.: Prentice-Hall, 1960. 239 p.

> A highly useful series of readings dealing with the major approaches to international relations, together with the editor's critiques and suggestions for new directions of research. Included are readings on international relations as a discipline, political realism, systems theory, the nature of conflict, equilibrium theory, and decision making.

30   Kaplan, Morton A., ed. NEW APPROACHES TO INTERNATIONAL RELATIONS. New York: St. Martin's Press, 1968. 518 p.

> A good collection of original writings illustrative of behavioral international relations theory and research in the 1960s. Several chapters consider the utility of quantitative methodologies; small group theory; the systems approach; computer explorations of the balance of power; game theory and bargaining; decision making; and alternative world futures.

Approaches to International Relations

31 Kindleberger, Charles P. POWER AND MONEY: THE POLITICS OF INTERNATIONAL ECONOMICS AND THE ECONOMICS OF INTERNATIONAL POLITICS. New York: Basic Books, 1970. 246 p.

   A succinct examination of the relationship between economics and politics as they impinge on governmental policy and international relations. The volume contains extended treatment of such issues as the multinational corporation and its implications for national sovereignty; the use and effectiveness of economic instruments of warfare; economic factors affecting imperialism; and the political dimensions of trade, payments, capital movement, and foreign aid.

32 Knorr, Klaus, and Rosenau, James N., eds. CONTENDING APPROACHES TO INTERNATIONAL POLITICS. Princeton, N.J.: Princeton University Press, 1969. 297 p.

   An anthology containing many excellent writings illustrative of qualitative and quantitative approaches to international relations research. Among the topics examined are the traditionalist-behavioralist controversy; the nature of theory; problems of methodology; the application of scientific method and its limitations in the study of international relations.

33 Knorr, Klaus, and Verba, Sidney, eds. THE INTERNATIONAL SYSTEM: THEORETICAL ESSAYS. Princeton, N.J.: Princeton University Press, 1961. 237 p.

   A good collection of writings treating a wide range of approaches to the study of international relations illustrative of the interests of scholars in the early 1960s. The volume contains chapters on problems of theory building and testing; gaming and bargaining theory; the level-of-analysis problem; alternative models of the international system; the nature of international crisis; and the role of law in the international system.

34 Kriesberg, Louis. SOCIAL PROCESSES IN INTERNATIONAL RELATIONS: A READER. New York: John Wiley and Sons, 1968. 577 p.

   An anthology containing twenty-nine writings illustrative of social science research of the 1960s. Among the topics examined are national stereotypes and foreign contact; international communication and legislative behavior; the professional soldier, political behavior, and coalition warfare; conflict behavior within and between nations; East-West interaction patterns; a simulation study of deterrence theories; and intercultural communication.

35 Lerche, Charles O., Jr., and Said, Abdul A. CONCEPTS OF INTERNATIONAL POLITICS. Englewood Cliffs, N.J.: Prentice-Hall, 1964. 314 p.

Approaches to International Relations

An introductory text that presents a conceptual framework focusing on the actors; the international system; and the major issues of international politics. Included are analyses on foreign policy, and on conflict and its regulation; the nature of war; ideology and world politics; the state system in transition; and new forms of organization beyond the nation-state.

36   Lieber, Robert J. THEORY AND WORLD POLITICS. Cambridge, Mass.: Winthrop Publishers, 1972. 166 p.

An analysis of five contemporary approaches to the study of international politics, including game theory, theories of integration, theories of power and conflict, cybernetics and communication theories, and systems theory. The volume contains a short bibliography of writings which provide a more comprehensive treatment of each of the theories examined.

37   McClelland, Charles A. THEORY AND THE INTERNATIONAL SYSTEM. New York: Macmillan Co., 1966. 138 p.

An examination of the role of theory in social science, the scope of international relations, the major interpretations and uses of the concepts of "power" and "influence," and the contribution of communication theory to the study of international relations. A major portion of the volume is devoted to systems analysis which, according to the author, provides a means of linking the various "islands" of theory, while contributing to an understanding of the major gaps in international relations theory.

38   McLellan, David S., et al., eds. THE THEORY AND PRACTICE OF INTERNATIONAL RELATIONS. 4th ed. Englewood Cliffs, N.J.: Prentice-Hall, 1974. 492 p.

A collection of writings from the recent literature focusing on major theories and their application to the practice of international relations. Included are essays on the actors in international politics; nationalism and internationalism; supra- and transnational actors; international organizations; capability analysis; foreign policy decision-making; diplomacy; propaganda; the threat and use of force; conflict management and resolution; alliance relationships; and international law.

39   Merritt, Richard L., and Rokkan, Stein, eds. COMPARING NATIONS: THE USE OF QUANTITATIVE DATA IN CROSS-NATIONAL RESEARCH. New Haven: Yale University Press, 1966. 584 p.

A volume containing chapters based on quantitative research undertaken, for the most part, in the early 1960s. Included are analyses of problems of data gathering and analysis on a cross-national basis; the use of aggregate data in

Approaches to International Relations

cross-national comparisons of differences within and among nations; and proposals for advancing quantitative comparative analysis. The volume contains a selected, but extensive, bibliography on cross-national research.

40   Morgan, Roger, ed. THE STUDY OF INTERNATIONAL AFFAIRS: ESSAYS IN HONOR OF KENNETH YOUNGER. New York: Oxford University Press, 1972. 309 p.

A collection of thirteen original essays examining the evolution of the study of international relations since the early twentieth century. Among the topics examined are human rights in international relations; the politics of cooperation and integration in Western Europe; international economic relationships; and relationships among nations in Eastern Europe, South Asia, Africa, and the British Commonwealth of Nations.

41   Morgenthau, Hans J. THE DECLINE OF DEMOCRATIC POLITICS. Chicago: University of Chicago Press, 1962. 431 p.

The first of three volumes containing important writings by the author previously published elsewhere (see Nos. 150 and 152). Included are selections dealing with such topics as the nature of international politics; international relations as an academic discipline; the separation of powers; nationalism; neutrality and neutralism; traditional and United Nations diplomacy; and the democratic process and foreign policy.

42   Mueller, John E., ed. APPROACHES TO MEASUREMENT IN INTERNATIONAL RELATIONS: A NON-EVANGELICAL SURVEY. New York: Appleton-Century-Crofts, 1969. 311 p.

An anthology of writings representative of the quantitative international relations literature. Included are chapters on the calculus of deterrence, the use of public opinion data, content analysis, mathematical and statistical models, voting patterns in international organizations, aggregate data, and bargaining games.

43   Paxton, John. THE STATESMAN'S YEAR-BOOK, 1974-1975. New York: St. Martin's Press, 1974. 1,556 p.

The most recent edition of a useful volume, published annually, containing information and statistics on the government, geography, population, religion, economy, currency and educational system of all countries, as well as data on world resources, including the sea bed. Each section contains bibliographies for further reading.

Approaches to International Relations

44 Platig, E. Raymond. INTERNATIONAL RELATIONS RESEARCH: PROBLEMS OF EVALUATION AND ADVANCEMENT. Santa Barbara, Calif.: Carnegie Endowment for International Peace, 1967. 211 p.

   A discussion of international relations as a developing social science discipline with emphasis on the functions and methods of research as they relate to theory building and policy formulation. The author provides propositions related to basic concepts in international relations, and develops criteria by which to judge the relevance of research, distinguishing among research for theory, history-oriented research, method-oriented research, and action-oriented research.

45 Porter, Brian, ed. INTERNATIONAL POLITICS: 1919-69. New York: Oxford University Press, 1972. 390 p.

   A collection of fifteen original chapters based on papers presented in 1969 in honor of the fiftieth anniversary of the founding of the world's first chair in International Politics at the University College of Wales. Included are essays on the evolution of international relations as a field of study; changes in diplomacy and in the use of force between 1919 and 1969; technology, economics, ideology, and nationalism; the growth of international institutions; the legal framework in a world of change; and morality in international politics.

46 Pruitt, Dean G., and Snyder, Richard D. THEORY AND RESEARCH ON THE CAUSES OF WAR. Englewood Cliffs, N.J.: Prentice-Hall, 1969. 314 p.

   An important behaviorally-oriented collection of writings based on contemporary research and theory by American scholars on the causes of war. Among the topics examined are motives and perceptions underlying the entry of nations into war; restraints against the use of violence; statistical data concerning the incidence of war; and efforts to create an integrated theory on the causes of war.

47 Puchala, Donald James. INTERNATIONAL POLITICS TODAY. New York: Dodd, Mead and Co., 1971. 379 p.

   A textbook for advanced undergraduate or basic graduate courses which incorporates theories, research, and findings from the social science literature of the 1960s. The author describes major approaches to international relations, including cybernetic modeling; presents a framework for political analysis; and examines such topics as public opinion and foreign policy, regional integration, the international politics of peace, power, nationalism, modernization, and arms control.

Approaches to International Relations

48 Pye, Lucian W., ed. POLITICAL SCIENCE AND AREA STUDIES: RIVALS OR PARTNERS? Bloomington: Indiana University Press, 1975. 245 p.

> A series of original essays whose authors, from a variety of contrasting perspectives, examine the place of area studies in political science and international relations. Together, the chapters set forth the unique features of each of the world's major regions, as well as the potential and limitations of efforts to transcend an area or country-specific focus in order to produce theories with more general applicability and validity.

49 Rapoport, Anatol, and Chammah, Albert M. PRISONER'S DILEMMA: A STUDY IN CONFLICT AND COOPERATION. Ann Arbor: University of Michigan Press, 1965. 258 p.

> An elaborate analysis of game theory and the exposition of a two-choice situation termed by the authors "prisoner's dilemma." The volume contains a mathematical theory of the game, together with results from the testing of the model.

50 Renouvin, Pierre, and Duroselle, Jean-Baptiste. INTRODUCTION TO THE HISTORY OF INTERNATIONAL RELATIONS. New York: Frederick A. Praeger, 1967. 432 p.

> An analysis focusing on major forces shaping international relations, including geography, demographic movements, economic interests, public opinion, and nationalism. Major attention is given to leadership, including principal typologies of personality, the perception of "national interest," and decision making. The volume contains an extensive, but selected, bibliography.

51 Rosecrance, Richard N. INTERNATIONAL RELATIONS: PEACE OR WAR? New York: McGraw-Hill Book Co., 1973. 334 p.

> A textbook for undergraduate use, bringing together the major approaches and propositions contained in recent international relations literature, with special emphasis on the conceptual frameworks and findings of quantitative research as well as the history of the international system. Included are chapters dealing with the nature, structure, and interaction of political systems, the evolution of diplomacy, military techniques, and the role of force, economic statecraft, and the prospects for peace and conflict, nationalism and internationalism, regionalism and globalism, in the evolving international system.

52 Rosenau, James N. INTERNATIONAL STUDIES AND THE SOCIAL SCIENCES: PROBLEMS, PRIORITIES AND PROSPECTS IN THE UNITED STATES. Beverly Hills, Calif.: Sage Library of Social Research, a division of Sage Publications, 1973. 147 p.

A report setting forth the results of a survey of a sample of
101 leading scholars which was designed to produce data about
the nature of the field of international studies, and which included the following topics: the career patterns, interests, and
training of scholars; patterns of association and communications;
attitudes toward area programs and the generation of knowledge;
views about teaching students, fostering public enlightenment,
and servicing the needs of government; the need for data and
data banks, and for achieving greater interdisciplinary corporation. The author presents the findings of the questionnaire as
well as his own assessment, based on the data assembled, about
the current state of international studies.

53   _____, ed. INTERNATIONAL POLITICS AND FOREIGN POLICY: A READER IN RESEARCH AND THEORY. Rev. ed. New York: Free Press, 1969. 740 p.

An impressive and useful collection of writings on theory and
methodology which includes selections on most of the contending approaches to the study of international relations, but
emphasizes the quantitative literature of the 1960s. Included
are selections on decision making, integration, strategic theory,
game theory, systems theory, field theory, learning theory,
capability analysis, and the nature and structure of the international system and its regional subsystems.

54   Rosenau, James N., et al., eds. THE ANALYSIS OF INTERNATIONAL POLITICS. New York: Free Press, 1972. 397 p.

A volume containing eighteen original essays in honor of Harold
and Margaret Sprout addressed to theoretical problems, conceptual foci, and empirical concerns of international politics as a
field of study. Among the topics examined are explanation,
prediction, and forecasting; policy classification; the analysis
of national capabilities; and sources of international conflict.

55   Russell, Frank Marion. THEORIES OF INTERNATIONAL RELATIONS. New York: D. Appleton-Century Co., 1936. 651 p.

A massive work which traces the development of relations
among groups and among nations from primitive man to ancient
China, India, Greece, Rome, Medieval Europe, and the Renaissance and the Reformation, as well as the modern nation-state
system. The author places emphasis on the study of international relations from the perspective of the 1930s, with extended treatment of pacifism, the League of Nations system, balance of power, nationalism and national minorities, imperialism
and disarmament. Because of its extensive documentation, the
volume has historiographic value.

56 Russett, Bruce M. POWER AND COMMUNITY IN WORLD POLITICS. San Francisco: W.H. Freeman and Co., 1974. 372 p.

> A collection of many of the author's writings over a twelve-year period. Included are essays on the environment of world politics; the nature of international violence; the deterrence of conflict; the instruments of influence and the limits of power; communications and international integration; and theories of alliance formation.

57 Said, Abdul [A.], ed. THEORY OF INTERNATIONAL RELATIONS: THE CRISIS OF RELEVANCE. Englewood Cliffs, N.J.: Prentice-Hall, 1968. 191 p.

> An anthology of original essays representative of theory-building efforts of the 1960s. Contributors address themselves to topics such as simulation and the building of international relations theory; communications and international relations theory; the impact of the cold war and the emergence of non-Western states on theories of international relations; and the implications of science and technology for the international system and for American foreign policy.

58 Scott, Andrew M. THE FUNCTIONING OF THE INTERNATIONAL POLITICAL SYSTEM. New York: Macmillan Co., 1967. 244 p.

> Utilizing systems analysis, the author sets forth in each chapter a series of linked propositions about major approaches to, and problems of, international relations. Included are propositional commentaries concerning images, values, and ideology; communication; decision making; conflict and collaboration; bargaining and negotiation; threat and deterrence; escalation and de-escalation; system change; and the international system in transition.

59 Shubik, Martin, ed. GAME THEORY AND RELATED APPROACHES TO SOCIAL BEHAVIOR: SELECTIONS. New York: John Wiley and Sons, 1964. 390 p.

> A collection of twenty-four writings on game theory which are representative, for the most part, of the literature of the 1950s. The anthology contains selections on such topics as mathematics and social analysis; the scaling of utility and probability; experimental games and bargaining theory; and the analysis of strategic choices.

60 Sills, David L., ed. INTERNATIONAL ENCYCLOPEDIA OF THE SOCIAL SCIENCES. 17 vols. New York: Macmillan Co., Free Press, 1968.

> A monumental work, reflecting the contributions of many social scientists, devoted to articles on concepts, theories, and meth-

ods in many disciplines, including the following: anthropology; economics; geography; history; law; political science; psychiatry; psychology; sociology; and statistics. In addition, the encyclopedia contains articles on major societies of the world as well as area studies.

61 Singer, J. David, ed. QUANTITATIVE INTERNATIONAL POLITICS. New York: Free Press, 1968. 394 p.

   A series of essays representative of the quantitative research of the 1960s, testing theories of conflict, integration, alliance formation and the outbreak of war, the relationship between national attributes and foreign conflict, social change and national aggressiveness, the delineation of international regions, and perceptions and reactions in crises.

62 Steinbruner, John D. THE CYBERNETIC THEORY OF DECISION: NEW DIMENSIONS OF POLITICAL ANALYSIS. Princeton, N.J.: Princeton University Press, 1974. 366 p.

   Drawing on cybernetic theory from such fields as information theory, behavioral psychology, and mathematical logic, the author develops a paradigm for the analysis of foreign policy decisions. The cybernetic paradigm is applied to the analysis of the politics of nuclear sharing in NATO between 1956 and 1964, with special emphasis on the multilateral force of the early 1960s.

63 Tanter, Raymond, and Ullman, Richard H., eds. THEORY AND POLICY IN INTERNATIONAL RELATIONS. Princeton, N.J.: Princeton University Press, 1972. 250 p.

   An excellent collection of writings assessing the utility and limitations of theories of international relations for policymakers. Included are essays on theories of bureaucratic politics; crisis diplomacy; the dynamics of international conflict; strategies of interdependence; and the problems of organizing information, theory, and knowledge to meet policy needs.

64 Thompson, Kenneth W. POLITICAL REALISM AND THE CRISIS OF WORLD POLITICS: AN AMERICAN APPROACH TO FOREIGN POLICY. Princeton, N.J.: Princeton University Press, 1960. 261 p.

   The author describes, synthesizes, and analyzes major realist theories and assesses their contribution to international relations. Realist theory is utilized in an examination of the problem of international morality, the operation of balance of power and collective security, U.S. national security policy, diplomacy, colonialism, and the prerequisites for a more peaceful world.

Approaches to International Relations

65   Toma, Peter A. UNDERSTANDING WORLD POLITICS. Notre Dame, Ind.: University of Notre Dame Press, 1975. 234 p.

   Building on realist writings of international relations, the author sets forth a framework for analyzing the world of the 1970s. Included are assessments of changing international patterns of relationships; the role of ideology in the contemporary world; and the reconciliation of idealism and realism in international politics and American foreign policy.

66   Toma, Peter A., et al., eds. BASIC ISSUES IN INTERNATIONAL RELATIONS. Boston: Allyn and Bacon, 1974. 594 p.

   A collection of forty-two writings designed for advanced undergraduate use. Included are selections on the scope and alternative approaches to the study of international relations; the international system and its actors; ends and means in foreign policy; international tension, conflict, and war; and the role of international organizations in world politics.

67   Wolfers, Arnold. DISCORD AND COLLABORATION: ESSAYS ON INTERNATIONAL POLITICS. Baltimore: Johns Hopkins Press, 1962. 283 p.

   A series of analyses and reflections on the nature of international relations, the pursuit of national security, and the role of power in the twentieth century. Among the topics examined are the determinants and goals of foreign policy; amity and hostility among nations; the balance of power in theory and practice; collective security; political theory and international relations; and the role of morality in the conduct of diplomacy among nations.

68   Wright, Quincy. THE STUDY OF INTERNATIONAL RELATIONS. New York: Appleton-Century-Crofts, 1955. 642 p.

   A major text containing an examination of the nature and history of international relations as a discipline; modes of analysis; the art of war; the conduct of foreign relations; international law and organization; and international economics. The author sets forth a "field theory" for the study of international relations that has had a seminal influence on more recent scholars.

69   Young, Oran R. THE INTERMEDIARIES: THIRD PARTIES IN INTERNATIONAL CRISES. Princeton, N.J.: Princeton University Press, 1967. 427 p.

   An examination of the conditions and roles of third party intermediaries in the termination of international crises based on a theoretical framework developed by the author. Included is an analysis of the nature and characteristics of international crises, and alternative types of third party intermediaries with special emphasis on the United Nations and its Secretary-General.

70 Zawodny, J.K. GUIDE TO THE STUDY OF INTERNATIONAL RELATIONS. San Francisco: Chandler Publishing Co., 1966. 151 p.

An annotated listing of major source materials, including abstracts, atlases, archives, bibliographies, periodicals, research in progress, statistics and other quantitative data, treaty collections, surveys of world events, yearbooks, and collections and libraries with holdings in international relations.

71 _____, ed. MAN AND INTERNATIONAL RELATIONS. 2 vols. San Francisco: Chandler Publishing Co., 1967. Vol. 1, 703 p.; vol. 2, 940 p.

A two-volume anthology of works on conflict (vol. 1) and integration (vol. 2), structured in three levels of analysis: individual psychodynamics, group dynamics, and nation-state relations. Included are more than 180 selections drawn from biology, sociology, psychology, psychiatry, anthology, political science, and international relations.

Chapter 3
THE NATURE OF THE INTERNATIONAL SYSTEM

Essential to the study of international relations is an understanding of the prospects for, and the limitations of, change in the international system. In fact, much of the literature of international relations seeks to identify those factors that are immutable and those that can be altered. Physical factors such as geography, natural resources, and climate are as important in shaping a nation's foreign policy as nonphysical factors such as ideology and nationalism.

Over the last two decades, there have emerged numerous theories about the nature of the international system. Scholars have chosen the international system as an important level of analysis in international relations. For example, Morton A. Kaplan, in a pioneering work on systems theory and international relations, devised six analytical models in order to examine the patterns of interaction in differing international environments.[1] Kaplan and other international relations scholars have developed models, within which relations among the constituent units are described with great accuracy. Models of international systems enable the scholar or policymaker to think conceptually. A world model based on balance of power or a particular form of world government provides the analyst with a general understanding of major patterns of interaction among the principal units. It is useful to compare the real world with the hypothetical worlds presented in models of the international system. In fact, most analyses of world affairs contain, implicitly at least, models of the international system. It is common to speak, for example, of a shift from the bipolarity of the early postwar period to a world of greater multipolarity. Implicit in bipolarity and multipolarity is a model of the international system based, respectively on two or a larger number of power centers.

Although the nature of the emerging multipolar international structure is uncertain, questions about the relationship between multipolarity and the potential for general or limited conflict, or between multipolarity and foreign policy choices,

---

[1]Morton A. Kaplan, SYSTEM AND PROCESS IN INTERNATIONAL RELATIONS (No. 94). See also No. 84.

have been discussed extensively in international relations literature. One hypothesis suggests that a multipolar world allows states a wider range of alternatives in pursuit of foreign policy objectives than does a bipolar international system.[2] Interaction among several power centers is alleged to result in crosscutting loyalties and a reduction in global tension and hostility. Other scholars have held that a bipolar system in which there is great disparity between the capabilities of the superpowers, on the one hand, and those of the lesser states, on the other hand, is better able than a multipolar world to restrict conflict and maintain stability.[3]

In addition, international relations scholars have turned increasingly to the study of historical international systems in their efforts to develop and validate propositions about relationships among nations and other actors. Such studies have included, for example, the analysis of those factors making for equilibrium and disturbance in a historical context.[4] Answers have been sought to questions such as the factors leading to a transformation from the international system of the late eighteenth century to the Napoleonic dominance of the early nineteenth century. While diplomatic historians have generally focused on studies of discrete periods and events, international relations scholars have attempted to discern recurring patterns within and among various international systems such as a classical balance of power, bipolarity or multipolarity.

Other scholars have sought to collect data about various patterns of interaction among nations and other groups into which the world is divided. As a means of studying more systematically relations among nations, data about trade, communications patterns, diplomatic relations, and the behavior of nations during periods of crisis have been collected as part of an effort to "map" more precisely the relationships among nations. Hypotheses about the propensity toward conflict in international systems based upon bipolarity or multipolarity have been tested by the utilization of data about wars and alliances at various times in the history of the international system.

The study of the international system has included the development of techniques for the study of the future and, specifically, for the designing of future worlds. Especially in the last decade, there have been many new studies whose authors propose methodologies for studying and anticipating the future as well as frame-

---

[2] Karl W. Deutsch and J. David Singer, "Multipolar Systems and International Stability," WORLD POLITICS 16 (April 1964), p. 390. See also Nos. 73, 78, 80, and 95.

[3] Kenneth N. Waltz, "International Structure, National Force, and the Balance of World Power," JOURNAL OF INTERNATIONAL AFFAIRS 21 (1967), pp. 215-31.

[4] See, for example, Richard N. Rosecrance, ACTION AND REACTION IN WORLD POLITICS (No. 112).

Nature of the International System

works for the conduct of relations among nations designed to minimize, or to avoid, the perceived ills of the present. The growth of interest in environmental problems, resource issues, population, and the propensity toward international conflict have contributed to the growth of such studies. They represent a continuation of, or a return to, a normative study of international relations which, as noted in the introduction to this volume, was of interest to earlier scholars of international relations.

Much of the study of international relations has consisted of the examination of major components of the international system. Scholars have had a continuing interest in the effects of such forces as ideology, nationalism, and technology upon relations among nations as well as the structure of the international system. The rise of nationalism transformed the international system of the nineteenth century to the global system of the late twentieth century. The effect of nationalism was to alter the boundaries of the old states of Europe and to bring about the end of empires such as Austria-Hungary in Europe as well as the worldwide empires of European states. The growth of ideologies, of great interest to scholars, had a profound effect upon the conduct of international relations in the twentieth century. It is unnecessary to belabor the importance of fascism and communism for the international system of the twentieth century.

While the principal focus of international relations has been upon the nation-state, larger numbers of scholars are recognizing the emergence of new nonstate actors whose activities are shaping the global system of the late twentieth century. Scholars have turned their attention to such nonstate actors as the multinational corporation, international terrorist groups, international organizations, and other groups whose activities are conducted often beyond the purview of the nation-state. It is not difficult to anticipate the continued emphasis of international relations upon the study of such forces and upon the development of methodologies and theories for their investigation. Nor is it difficult to predict that the models of the international system that evolve in the years ahead in the literature of international relations will give a greater place to the new actors of international relations.

72   Arendt, Hannah. THE ORIGINS OF TOTALITARIANISM. New York: Meridian Books, 1960. 520 p.

> A perceptive analysis of the origins of twentieth-century totalitarianism based on extended treatment of anti-Semitism in European history; the expansion of the nation-state; nationalism; and imperialism. Major attention is given to the role of ideology, propaganda, organization, and the secret police in totalitarian movements.

73   Aron, Raymond. PEACE AND WAR: A THEORY OF INTERNATIONAL RELATIONS. Garden City, N.Y.: Doubleday and Co., 1966. 820 p.

> A monumental survey of the nature of international systems past and present, the meaning of power, bipolarity and multipolarity, the causes of war, the role of diplomacy, economics, and geo-

Nature of the International System

graphic factors in world politics. The analysis contained in this important volume is divided into theory, sociology, history, and "praxeology"; these form four overlapping levels of conceptualization in Aron's work.

74 Axline, W. Andrew, and Stegenga, James A. THE GLOBAL COMMUNITY: A BRIEF INTRODUCTION TO INTERNATIONAL RELATIONS. New York: Dodd, Mead and Co., 1972. 196 p.

A text designed for use at an elementary college level that deals, in pessimistic and apocalyptic terms, with the present state of world politics, together with the authors' prescriptions for the future. Included are chapters dealing with the state and foreign policy, the international system, the nature of international tensions and conflict management, and the struggle for world order.

75 Bell, Daniel, ed. TOWARD THE YEAR 2000: WORK IN PROGRESS. Boston: Houghton-Mifflin Co., 1968. 400 p.

A volume containing memoranda and essays produced by the Commission on the Year 2000 established by the American Academy of Arts and Sciences. The contributors address themselves to such topics as the methodology of futurology and technological forecasting; planning and predicting; higher education; biological war, the life cycle, and the year 2000; violence; the relationship between federal and local government; and religion and the institutional church.

76 Black, Cyril E., et al. NEUTRALIZATION AND WORLD POLITICS. Princeton, N.J.: Princeton University Press, 1968. 195 p.

In seven interrelated essays, the authors examine the nature and potential uses of neutralization in the contemporary world. Included are analyses of neutralization in historical perspective; areas suitable for neutralization; and the problems of negotiating neutralization.

77 Bozeman, Adda B. POLITICS AND CULTURE IN INTERNATIONAL HISTORY. Princeton, N.J.: Princeton University Press, 1960. 560 p.

An impressive study of ancient civilizations in the Middle East, India, Greece, Rome, and China, with special emphasis on their relations with other peoples. The author draws on findings about relations among peoples in ancient times to assess contemporary international affairs.

78 Buchan, Alastair. THE END OF THE POSTWAR ERA: A NEW BALANCE OF WORLD POWER. New York: Saturday Review Press, a division of E.P. Dutton and Co., 1974. 347 p.

Nature of the International System

A survey of the evolution of the international system in the early 1970s with emphasis on the transition from the postwar bipolarity to a world of additional power centers. Included are analyses of American foreign policy and the Nixon Doctrine; the rise to importance of new issue areas such as energy and raw materials; the nature of global interdependence; the foreign policies of the Soviet Union, China, Japan, and the nations of Western Europe; and the prospects for multilateral power balance.

79 Carr, E.H. NATIONALISM AND AFTER. London: Macmillan and Co., 1945. 74 p.

A short essay examining the origins and evolution of nationalism focusing on its impact on the international economic system of the early twentieth century. The author assesses the prospects for nationalism and for the emergence of a global community.

80 Crabb, Cecil V., Jr. NATIONS IN A MULTIPOLAR WORLD. New York: Harper and Row, 1968. 702 p.

An introductory textbook based on a framework for the analysis of a world of several power centers, in contrast to the bipolar configuration of international politics of the postwar generation. The author surveys the nature of national power; nationalism; diplomacy; international law and organization; disarmament and arms control; and the foreign policies of major powers.

81 Deutsch, Karl W. NATIONALISM AND SOCIAL COMMUNICATION: AN INQUIRY INTO THE FOUNDATIONS OF NATIONALITY. Cambridge, Mass.: MIT Press, 1966. 345 p.

Utilizing both quantitative and qualitative methodologies and approaches from several disciplines, the author develops a theory of nationalism and nation-building. Deutsch's theory incorporates such phenomena as communication patterns, social learning, preferences, the spread of national consciousness, social mobilization, and the contribution of elite groups to the growth of nationalism.

82 Emerson, Rupert. FROM EMPIRE TO NATION: THE RISE TO SELF-ASSERTION OF ASIAN AND AFRICAN PEOPLES. Boston: Beacon Press, 1960. 466 p.

A survey of the evolution of nationalism in the non-Western world. Included are analyses of the nature of the nation, colonial policy and national movements, nationalism and democracy, the erosion of democracy in new states; the principle of self-determination; and the role of new states in the international community.

83 Falk, Richard A. A STUDY OF FUTURE WORLDS. New York: Free Press, 1975. 506 p.

An analysis of what the author defines as global problems--the elimination of war, poverty, social injustice, and ecological instability--together with a framework and timetable for global solutions based on a reformed and integrated world polity. Included are chapters on the nature of values and value change; illustrations of principal types of world order systems; the evolving global economy; and the implications of the author's proposals for the United States.

84 Fliess, Peter J. THUCYDIDES AND THE POLITICS OF BIPOLARITY. Baton Rouge: Louisiana State University Press, 1966. 194 p.

A study of relations among Greek states before and during the Peloponnesian War. With terminology, analytic approaches, and analogies utilized in describing the modern international system, the author examines the development of alliances, power balances, neutrality, and imperial expansion in ancient Greece. Major attention is devoted to the impact of domestic affairs on foreign policy and the impact of foreign policy on domestic affairs in Athens and Sparta.

85 Gabor, Dennis. INVENTING THE FUTURE. New York: Alfred A. Knopf, 1964. 238 p.

The author analyzes existing and potential problems for mankind posed by the destructive power of modern weapons, the growth of population, natural resources shortages, and the emergence of a more leisure-oriented society. Emphasis is placed on the relationship among such problems, the challenges posed for mankind, and the prospects for the world of the late twentieth century.

86 Goodwin, Geoffrey L., and Linklater, Andrew, eds. NEW DIMENSIONS OF WORLD POLITICS. New York: Halsted Press, 1975. 127 p.

A collection of six essays, published in this volume for the first time, dealing with the role of nonstate actors and new forces in an increasingly interdependent system. Included are chapters on transnational and transgovernmental relations and the problems of world order in light of the growing importance of trade and monetary issues; population; and the management and conservation of natural resources.

87 Hekhius, Dale J., et al., eds. INTERNATIONAL STABILITY: MILITARY, ECONOMIC AND POLITICAL DIMENSIONS. New York: John Wiley and Sons, 1964. 296 p.

A collection of twelve essays, several of which were published for the first time in this volume, dealing with the then emerging international environment of the late 1960s. Included are analyses of the nature of change in less developed countries, the problem of military stability and deterrence, integration in Western Europe, peacekeeping, and arms control.

88   Herz, John H. INTERNATIONAL POLITICS IN THE ATOMIC AGE. New York: Columbia University Press, 1959. 360 p.

An analysis focusing on the impact of technology, and especially atomic weapons, on the modern state system, and the nation-state itself. The author assesses the nature and structure of bipolarity, the deterrence of conflict, collective security, and the future prospects for international politics.

89   Holsti, K.J. INTERNATIONAL POLITICS: A FRAMEWORK FOR ANALYSIS. 2d ed. Englewood Cliffs, N.J.: Prentice-Hall, 1972. 532 p.

A textbook whose focus is the nature of the international system within which states operate and the ways in which--and the purposes for which--states conduct their foreign policies. Drawing on recent research, the author examines major approaches to the study of international politics, and devotes major consideration to foreign policy outputs, including orientations and national roles; military capabilities and influence; diplomatic bargaining; propaganda; economic instruments; law and world opinion; conflict; conflict resolution; and major forms of collaboration among states. Included is an analysis of the evolution of international systems from the Chou Dynasty of 1122 B.C. to the twentieth century.

90   Huntington, Ellsworth. CIVILIZATION AND CLIMATE. New Haven: Yale University Press, 1915. 333 p.

An older analysis of the effect of climatic factors on civilization based on data collected by the author on population distribution, productivity, and temperature changes. Included is an examination of the nature of the "ideal" climate, as well as an assessment of shifts in climatic zones on historic civilizations.

91   _____. MAINSPRINGS OF CIVILIZATION. New York: John Wiley and Sons, 1945. 660 p.

An examination of cultural, biological, and environmental factors in shaping historical evolution and the growth of civilizations. In a volume that synthesizes and summarizes his earlier works, the author traces geographic patterns of civilization, describes phases of climatic cycles, and assesses the interplay of culture and heredity.

Nature of the International System

92 James, Alan, ed. THE BASES OF INTERNATIONAL ORDER: ESSAYS IN HONOR OF C.A.W. MANNING. New York: Oxford University Press, 1973. 218 p.

> A collection of eight original essays dealing with such topics as order and change in international society; the balance of power; the role of morality in international relations; the new states in the contemporary global system; and international law and organization. Included is an analysis of the contribution of theories of international relations to an understanding of the contemporary world.

93 Kahn, Herman, and Bruce-Biggs, B. THINGS TO COME: THINKING ABOUT THE 70'S AND 80'S. New York: Macmillan Co., 1972. 262 p.

> A methodological framework, incorporating techniques and assumptions of futurology and policy research, designed to provide an understanding of problems likely to confront the United States, domestically and internationally, in the next decade. The authors set forth multifold trends and surprise-free projections for the 1970s and 1980s, and assess likely technological innovations, sources of stability and instability, and the emerging postindustrial society.

94 Kaplan, Morton A. SYSTEM AND PROCESS IN INTERNATIONAL RELATIONS. New York: John Wiley and Sons, 1957. 283 p.

> In a pioneering work, the author develops six international relations models based on the following: a balance of power system; a loose, bipolar system; tight bipolarity; a hierarchical system; a world federal system; and a unit veto, or modern multipolar, system. The models provide a theoretical framework within which hypotheses can be generated and tested. Each hypothetical system contains five sets of variables: the essential rules, transformation rules, the actor classificatory variables, capability variables, and information variables.

95 Kissinger, Henry A. A WORLD RESTORED: THE POLITICS OF CONSERVATISM IN A REVOLUTIONARY AGE. New York: Grosset and Dunlap, 1964. 354 p.

> In a volume providing important insights into his conception of international politics and foreign policy, the author sets forth and analyzes a framework for international order based on "legitimacy." The conceptualization is utilized in the examination of the role and limits of diplomacy as well as the formation and dissolution of coalitions in Europe in 1815, at the time of the Congress of Vienna.

96 Kohn, Hans. THE AGE OF NATIONALISM: THE FIRST ERA OF GLOBAL HISTORY. New York: Harper and Brothers, 1962. 172 p.

Building on earlier research and writing, the author surveys the impact of nationalism on Europe since the French Revolution and assesses its implications for Afro-Asian states. Principal emphasis is placed on nationalism as a catalyst for the global awakening of peoples and the growth of international interdependence.

97 _____. THE IDEA OF NATIONALISM: A STUDY OF ITS ORIGINS AND BACKGROUND. New York: Macmillan Co., 1960. 735 p.

A comprehensive and important survey of the rise of nationalism and an analysis of nationalism in its various manifestations. The author traces the idea of nationalism from Old Testament Israel to ancient Greece and Rome, and during the Renaissance and Reformation. However, the major portion of the volume is devoted to modern nationalism, including the concept of the sovereign nation, and a comparative analysis of nationalism in England, France, Russia, Germany, Spain, Austria-Hungary, and Italy before the twentieth century.

98 Kothari, Rajni. FOOTSTEPS INTO THE FUTURE: DIAGNOSIS OF THE PRESENT WORLD AND A DESIGN FOR AN ALTERNATIVE. New York: Free Press, 1975. 173 p.

An Indian scholar's perspective on and critique of theories of modernization and the contemporary global system, together with proposals for the creation of an alternative world structure. The author examines problems of economic and social inequality and the nature of violence, and suggests strategies for change to the new world system that he describes.

99 Lepawsky, Albert, et al., eds. THE SEARCH FOR WORLD ORDER. New York: Appleton-Century-Crofts, 1971. 451 p.

This festschrift of twenty-six essays in honor of Quincy Wright is broadly focused on evolving legal, political, and organizational relationships between nation-states and the international system. Among the topics examined by a distinguished group of scholars are the nature of war; the sociology of strategic thinking; human rights and threats to peace; linkages between national politics and international politics; field theory and system theory; transnational patterns and phenomena; and the evolution of cross-disciplinary and scientific studies in political science and international relations.

100 Manning, C.A.W. THE NATURE OF INTERNATIONAL SOCIETY. New York: John Wiley and Sons, 1962. 220 p.

A philosophical treatment of the "social cosmos" which, ac-

Nature of the International System

cording to the author, is based on the interplay of myth and reality, of theory and practice, of form and substance. Included is a discussion of the nature of abstractions such as the nation and state, the role of theory, the significance of law, the bases of international compliance, and the competition for influence among nation-states.

101 Martin, Laurence W., ed. NEUTRALISM AND NONALIGNMENT: THE NEW STATES IN WORLD AFFAIRS. New York: Frederick A. Praeger, 1962. 249 p.

An analysis of the nature of neutralism and nonalignment in the context of the generation after World War II based on essays by eleven contributors, including the editors. The volume contains writings on such topics as the rationale for nonalignment; the neutralism of first generation leaders of new states; and the policies of nonaligned states in the United Nations.

102 Mates, Leo. NONALIGNMENT: THEORY AND CURRENT POLICY. Dobbs Ferry, N.Y.: Oceana Publications, 1972. 543 p.

Drawing on his experience as a Yugoslav diplomat, the author traces the origins of nonalignment and assesses its operation since World War II. Included are analyses of the decolonization process and the emergence of new states; the sociopolitical characteristics of social and economic development; the evolution of the Yugoslav policy of nonalignment; and new trends in the late 1960s affecting patterns and policies of nonalignment.

103 Meadows, Davis L., and Meadows, Donella H., eds. TOWARD GLOBAL EQUILIBRIUM: COLLECTED PAPERS. Cambridge, Mass.: Wright-Allen Press, 1973. 358 p.

A collection of thirteen papers exploring the nature and implications of physical growth on planet earth. In addition to developing a model of economic development and population growth, the contributors assess causes and consequences of growth as well as the problems and determinants of long-term resource availability.

104 Meadows, Donella H., et al. THE LIMITS TO GROWTH. New York: Universe Books, 1972. 205 p.

An analysis by an interdisciplinary, international group of policymakers, educators, and industrialists, the so-called Club of Rome, who address themselves to challenges facing mankind as a result of growing interdependence within the global international system. Included is an examination of the nature and limits of exponential growth, the impact of technology on in-

Nature of the International System

ternational politics, and the problems of achieving global equilibrium.

105 Mendlovitz, Saul H., ed. ON THE CREATION OF A JUST WORLD ORDER: PREFERRED WORLDS FOR THE 1990'S. New York: Free Press, 1975. 302 p.

Several scholars from Africa, China, India, Japan, Latin America, the United States, and Western Europe set forth their views concerning a preferred world of the year 2000. Included are normative analyses focused on cultural integration, global institutions, world order values, the control of violence, and the distribution of power and wealth among nations and between national actors and larger units.

106 Morgenthau, Hans J. POLITICS AMONG NATIONS: THE STRUGGLE FOR POWER AND PEACE. 5th ed. New York: Alfred A. Knopf, 1973. 617 p.

A leading textbook in which the author develops realist theory and sets forth a conception of international politics as a struggle for power. Much of this important volume is devoted to an analysis of the elements of national power, the role of balance of power in limiting conflict, and the conditions for the development of a world state. Included are chapters on international law and organization, diplomacy, imperialism, war, disarmament, and nationalism.

107 Niebuhr, Reinhold. THE STRUCTURE OF NATIONS AND EMPIRES. New York: Charles Scribner's Sons, 1959. 306 p.

A leading twentieth-century theologian describes recurring problems and patterns of international order, and focuses on the Soviet-American confrontation in the nuclear age. In his study of international relations, the author examines the nature of modern imperialism, the operation and failures of collective security, and the character of the modern nation-state, and evaluates the destructive and creative potential inherent in human freedom and in man.

108 Odell, Peter R. OIL AND WORLD POWER: BACKGROUND TO THE OIL CRISIS. New York: Taplinger Publishing Co., 1975. 245 p.

An examination of the role of oil in the emerging global power structure, with emphasis on the policies of major oil producing and consuming countries. The author examines the nature of the world's oil industry, as well as the role of oil in economic development and international relations after the October 1973 war in the Middle East.

Nature of the International System

109 Ogburn, William Fielding, ed. TECHNOLOGY AND INTERNATIONAL RELATIONS. Chicago: University of Chicago Press, 1949. 202 p.

   A series of nine essays in which the authors assess the implications for international relations of technological innovation in civilian and military technology. The volume includes chapters on such topics as the process of adjustment to new inventions, atomic energy, aviation, mass-communications, and the effects of modern technology on world order.

110 Palmer, Norman D., and Perkins, Howard C. INTERNATIONAL RELATIONS: THE WORLD COMMUNITY IN TRANSITION. 3d ed. Boston: Houghton Mifflin Co., 1969. 799 p.

   A basic text designed to provide a balanced introduction to the principles, instruments, institutions, and techniques of international relations, as well as contemporary world politics. Included are chapters on the management of power, diplomacy, international organization, the nature of national interest, the foreign policies of major powers, and conflict and change in each of the world's regions.

111 Pfaltzgraff, Robert L., Jr., ed. POLITICS AND THE INTERNATIONAL SYSTEM. 2d ed. Philadelphia: J.B. Lippincott Co., 1972. 614 p.

   An anthology of forty-two writings from the traditional and contemporary literature of international politics which focuses on the following topics: international relations as a discipline; the nature of the international system; conflict and military potential; technology and international politics; man-milieu relationships; domestic-international linkages; and the management of power. Included are selections on such topics as the realist-utopian debate; behavioralism and traditionalism; the level-of-analysis problem; nationalism; power as a concept; imperialism; the balance of terror; arms control; and international integration.

112 Rosecrance, Richard N. ACTION AND REACTION IN WORLD POLITICS. Boston: Little, Brown and Co., 1963. 314 p.

   European history from 1740 to 1960 is divided into nine periods or international systems. In an important and impressive effort to assess uniformities and differences within and among systems, the author identifies and examines disturbance inputs; regulator mechanisms that react to disturbances; environmental restraints influencing the range of possible outcomes; and the outcomes themselves.

Nature of the International System

113 Russett, Bruce M., et al. WORLD HANDBOOK OF POLITICAL AND SOCIAL INDICATORS. New Haven: Yale University Press, 1964. 373 p.

> A compilation of data on human resources, government, and politics, including the following: communications, wealth, education, social patterns, health, and religion. The data are presented to facilitate cross-national analysis of trends and patterns in international relations and comparative politics. Includes discussions of population and its characteristics, GNP and spending in the public sector, newspaper circulation, life expectancy, and employment in industry and agriculture.

114 Schwarzenberger, Georg. POWER POLITICS: A STUDY OF WORLD SOCIETY. 3d ed. New York: Frederick A. Praeger, 1964. 614 p.

> An examination of international relations as a discipline, the elements of power, the evolution of international society, the nation-state, the role and operation of international law and organization, and the conditions for world order. Included is an assessment of the operations of both the League of Nations and the United Nations within an international system based on power politics.

115 Sprout, Harold, and Sprout, Margaret. TOWARD A POLITICS OF THE PLANET EARTH. New York: Van Nostrand Reinhold Co., 1971. 499 p.

> A revised edition of a major text that examines the nature of the contemporary international system, sources of national policies and capabilities, and the forces making for change in the world of the 1970s. The authors place special emphasis on environmental and ecological factors and perspectives as well as the impact of technology, population growth, and resource needs on the contemporary international system. Included are analyses of the nature of power; foreign policy goals and their styles and strategies; geopolitical theories in ecological perspective; nationalism; international institutions and transnational norms; and forces making for global interdependence.

116 Strausz-Hupé, Robert, and Hazard, Harry W., eds. THE IDEA OF COLONIALISM. New York: Frederick A. Praeger, 1958. 496 p.

> A collection of fifteen original essays on colonialism both in its historical dimension and in the decade following World War II. The volume includes writings comparing the colonial policies and experiences of major powers such as Britain, France, Japan, and the United States, as well as analyses of imperial Tsarist and Communist Russian policies, the United Nations and colonialism, Indian attitudes toward colonialism, and anticolonialism in Latin America.

Nature of the International System

117 Strausz-Hupé, Robert, and Possony, Stefan T. INTERNATIONAL RELATIONS IN THE AGE OF CONFLICT BETWEEN DEMOCRACY AND DICTATORSHIP. 2d ed. New York: McGraw-Hill Book Co., 1954. 826 p.

    An extensive study in the form of a textbook of international relations. The volume includes an analysis of the nature and elements of power; theories and the conduct of foreign policy; international economics; imperialism and colonialism; and the role and limitations of international organizations in the quest for a more peaceful world.

118 Sullivan, David S., and Sattler, Martin J., eds. CHANGE AND THE FUTURE INTERNATIONAL SYSTEM. New York: Columbia University Press, 1972. 109 p.

    A collection of essays examining major forces shaping the world of the 1970s. While great emphasis is given to the impact of technological change on the international system and on international organization, several contributors address themselves to other issues: population, resources, ideology, and race. Among the contributors are Bernard Brodie, Robert C. North, Nazli Choucri, Herbert S. Dinerstein, Eugene B. Skolnikoff, William D. Coplin, Tilden J. LeMelle, and George W. Shepherd, Jr.

119 Van Dyke, Vernon. INTERNATIONAL POLITICS. New York: Appleton-Century-Crofts, 1966. 527 p.

    A basic text in which international politics is analyzed within the framework of an analogy with domestic politics. Included are analyses of the nature of politics, violence, security, nationalism, and war, as well as an assessment of the balance of power, diplomacy, economic factors, arms control, and international organization.

Chapter 4

FOREIGN POLICY AND DIPLOMACY

The study of the foreign policies of nations and the interaction of foreign policies constitutes a crucially important part of international relations as a field. Scholars have long sought to understand the nature of foreign policy and to develop normative standards against which to evaluate the foreign policies of nations. In realist literature, the concept of national interest was central to the study of foreign policy. In the writings of the utopian school, foreign policies were often evaluated in accordance with their correspondence with the norms set forth in international law and organization. Although there is a vast literature consisting of case studies on one or more aspects of the foreign policies of most nations, for at least the past decade there has been a growing interest among scholars in the development of frameworks for the study of foreign policy on a more comparative and systematic basis.

While earlier writers, especially those of the realist school, were often comparative--both among nations and between historical periods--they lacked, according to their critics, an adequate understanding of the motivations, perceptions, bureaucratic relationships, and values of decision makers. In the late 1950s, scholars began to develop conceptual frameworks for decision-making analysis. Such conceptualization emphasized the role of domestic and international influences, as well as such variables as personalities, predispositions, cultural backgrounds, and perceptions of decision makers in foreign policy decision making. Such analysis represented a shift in emphasis away from the study of national goals based on abstract conceptions of the state-as-actor toward an investigation of the perceptions, motivations, bureaucratic constraints, and roles of decision makers who act on behalf of the state.

Decision-making frameworks are illustrative of the effort to be both comparative and systematic in the study of foreign policy. The attempt to conceptualize and study international-domestic "linkages" represents yet another dimension of recent foreign policy studies.[1] This emphasis includes the study of the impact

---

[1] See James N. Rosenau, ed., LINKAGE POLITICS (No. 163). See also Nos. 152, 154, and 156.

of international forces on the domestic political structure of countries and their implications, in turn, for foreign policy. To a greater extent than ever before, the domestic structures of states are affected by developments beyond their national frontiers, over which they have little or no control. Moreover, change, such as a coup or revolution, within one country may, by "demonstration effect," help to trigger a similar phenomenon in another country. Thus the process by which international-domestic linkages occur is of great interest to contemporary scholars. Efforts have been made to develop and make use of theories based on international-domestic "linkages" in the comparative study of foreign policy.

The quest for a more systematic study of foreign policy has contributed to interest in data banks upon which scholars can draw for information on a large number of nations regarding, for example, diplomatic exchanges; behavior during crises; trade and other economic data; and military capabilities. Such scholars have concerned themselves with problems of conceptualization, measurement, reliability and validity of their findings, and prediction. Because the comparative and quantitative study of foreign policy remains in an early stage, there has been a considerable preoccupation with issues of conceptualization and methodology. Propositional inventories about foreign policy behavior have been developed. Scholars have addressed themselves to questions about the process and structure of foreign policy decision making; the relationship between a country's domestic political system and its foreign policy; the role of perceptual variables in foreign policy choice; and interest groups, public opinion, mass communications, voting behavior, and foreign policy.

In addition to problems of conceptualization and methodology, quantitatively-oriented scholars have produced studies based on categorization, volume, and analysis of data concerning transactions and events between pairs of nations, and among groups of nations. Scholars have addressed themselves to such questions as the extent to which recurring sequences and patterns of events between and among nations can be discerned, and their meaning both in analyzing and predicting the foreign policy behavior of a nation, or groups of nations.[2]

Historically, nation-states have employed a variety of means in the pursuit of national goals, including military force, economic sanctions, and diplomacy. A major part of the foreign policy of nations consists of efforts to adjust differences and to reconcile competing, or conflicting, national interests. The way in which diplomacy is utilized for this purpose has been of continuing interest to international relations scholars. A leading twentieth-century student and diplomatist, Harold Nicolson, defined diplomacy as the management of international relations by negotiation.[3] The success of diplomacy depends on many factors,

---

[2] See, for example, Nos. 138, 145, 146, 155, and 161.

[3] Harold Nicolson, DIPLOMACY (No. 154), p. 5. See also Nos. 121, 124, 131, 132, 135, 137, 141, 144, 170, and 172.

Foreign Policy and Diplomacy

including the power, values, attitudes, and conceptions of national interest held by national decision makers and public opinion in countries.

Scholars have compared and contrasted the role of diplomacy in differing international systems, and the use of diplomacy by democratic and totalitarian governments. The speeding of communications, the development of a global international system, and the increasing interdependence of nations have made far more complex the conduct of relations among nations. Because nations must grapple with problems that have existed for a long time, at the same time responding to new challenges, the study of diplomacy and its effective utilization will be of continuing interest to scholars and practitioners in shaping the world of the future.

120 Allison, Graham T. ESSENCE OF DECISION: EXPLAINING THE CUBAN MISSILE CRISIS. Boston: Little, Brown and Co., 1971. 338 p.

> A seminal and important volume setting forth a framework for the analysis of foreign policy decisions by means of three models: the rational-actor model, focusing on foreign policy goals and interests; the organizational model, dealing with the influence of structured units on decision making; and the bureaucratic model, emphasizing the interests, perceptions, differences, and patterns of interaction among those participating in a decision-making process. Each of these models is utilized to analyze American and Soviet decision making during the Cuban missile crisis.

121 Bailey, Thomas A. THE ART OF DIPLOMACY: THE AMERICAN EXPERIENCE. New York: Appleton-Century-Crofts, 1968. 303 p.

> An analysis of American diplomacy in which the author sets forth 267 basic guidelines, or maxims, and illustrates them by historical examples. Included are chapters on the president as chief diplomat; policy formulation and diplomacy; diplomatic techniques; war and diplomacy; and the perils of peacemaking.

122 Beard, Charles A. THE IDEA OF NATIONAL INTEREST: AN ANALYTICAL STUDY IN AMERICAN FOREIGN POLICY. New York: Macmillan Co., 1934. 583 p.

> An analytical and descriptive study of the concept of national interest, with special emphasis on the American experience. Included are such topics as national interest in territorial expansion; the economic components of national interest; illustrations of national interest in action; and the means by which national interest has been advanced and enforced.

123 Butterfield, Herbert. THE STATECRAFT OF MACHIAVELLI. London: G. Bell and Sons, 1960. 167 p.

Foreign Policy and Diplomacy

An examination of the cult of antiquity, the use of the inductive method, and the political ethics upon which Machiavelli's statecraft was based. The author assesses the influence of Machiavelli on later scholars, especially in England.

124 Clark, Eric. DIPLOMAT: THE WORLD OF INTERNATIONAL DIPLOMACY. New York: Taplinger Publishing Co., 1974. 276 p.

A survey of the nature of diplomacy, and the changing role of the diplomat, in the present world with special emphasis on the impact of rapid communications, the growth of propaganda, and the effects of the cold war on diplomatic practice. Basing his book on extensive interviews with diplomats from several countries, the author discusses evolving patterns of diplomatic recruitment and training; the embassy and reporting; contrasts between communist and noncommunist diplomats; and the role of diplomacy at the United Nations.

125 Cohen, Bernard C. THE PRESS AND FOREIGN POLICY. Princeton, N.J.: Princeton University Press, 1963. 288 p.

A perceptive study of the relationship between the press and foreign policy with special emphasis on the definition by the press of its role and its impact on policymaking and public opinion. Included are analyses of the policymakers' views of the press and the utilization of news by those making foreign policy decisions.

126 Cook, Thomas I., and Moos, Malcolm. POWER THROUGH PURPOSE: THE REALISM OF IDEALISM AS A BASIS FOR FOREIGN POLICY. Baltimore: Johns Hopkins Press, 1954. 216 p.

An excellent analysis of the postwar bipolar setting for U.S. foreign policy, the nature of Soviet and American goals and national interest, and the historic foundations of U.S. idealism. Contending that neither isolationism nor power politics provides in itself an adequate basis for foreign policy, the authors develop a conception of an internationalist national interest. They set forth guidelines for American foreign policy based on a reconciliation between idealism and realism underwritten by adequate national capabilities.

127 Davison, W. Phillips. INTERNATIONAL POLITICAL COMMUNICATION. New York: Frederick A. Praeger, 1965. 404 p.

An assessment of the effects of communications on individuals and groups and the role of the mass media in the foreign policy of the United States and other countries. The author examines international communications on a government-to-people, and on a people-to-people basis.

128 de Rivera, Joseph H. THE PSYCHOLOGICAL DIMENSION OF FOREIGN POLICY. Columbus, Ohio: Charles E. Merrill Publishing Co., 1968. 441 p.

> An effort to utilize contemporary psychology in the study of foreign policy decision making and to suggest areas in which further research in psychology might enrich our understanding of foreign policy. The focus of the volume is on such topics as decision makers' perceptions and construction of reality; the constraints on action; selective biases; decisions in the context of the organization; the dynamics of interaction within small groups as decisional units; the interpretation of messages; and psychological aspects of consensus formation within decision-making organizations in the U.S. government.

129 Eubank, Keith. THE SUMMIT CONFERENCES, 1919-1960. Norman: University of Oklahoma Press, 1966. 225 p.

> An analysis of the strengths and weaknesses, the problems and pitfalls, of summit diplomacy based on a comparative study of conferences in the interwar years and in the postwar period. Included are examinations of the Versailles Conference, Munich, Teheran, Yalta, Geneva, and the abortive Paris summit meeting of 1960.

130 Frankel, Joseph. THE MAKING OF FOREIGN POLICY: AN ANALYSIS OF DECISION-MAKING. New York: Oxford University Press, 1963. 231 p.

> The author sets forth a decision-making model in which the environment, communications, values, and information play a crucial role in the policy process. Included is an analysis of the role of various groups within the government, public opinion, political parties and interest groups, and concepts of national interest and rationality in the formation of foreign policy.

131 Halperin, Morton H. BUREAUCRATIC POLITICS AND FOREIGN POLICY. Washington, D.C.: Brookings Institution, 1974. 340 p.

> An analysis of the role of bureaucratic groups and interests in the formulation of American foreign policy. Utilizing materials not only from the memoirs of high officials, but also interviews with lesser members of the U.S. government, past and present, together with his own experience, the author examines propositions about bureaucratic behavior by reference to specific cases. Included are chapters devoted to the discussion of bureaucratic perceptions of national interest; the exercise of influence within a bureaucracy; the uses of the press; the planning of decisional strategy; and problems of presidential control.

Foreign Policy and Diplomacy

132   Harr, John Ensor. THE PROFESSIONAL DIPLOMAT. Princeton, N.J.: Princeton University Press, 1969. 404 p.

>   A study of the impact of the "new diplomacy" on diplomatic establishments, with special emphasis on the United States Foreign Service as a case study. The book includes an analysis of personnel requirements; the use of new management techniques; the multifaceted nature of diplomacy in the contemporary world; and the social origins, characteristics, and composition of the United States Foreign Service.

133   Hayter, William. THE DIPLOMACY OF THE GREAT POWERS. New York: Macmillan Co., 1961. 75 p.

>   A short survey, based on the author's personal experience as a British diplomat, of diplomacy as practiced by the United States, the Soviet Union, France, and Britain, together with general observations on diplomatic method.

134   Hermann, Charles F. CRISES IN FOREIGN POLICY: A SIMULATION ANALYSIS. Indianapolis and New York: Bobbs-Merrill Co., 1969. 234 p.

>   A volume which reviews the literature of international crises setting forth a definition of crisis and a simulation model that utilizes a decision-making framework. In a simulation exercise based on elements of the U.S. decision to resist the invasion of South Korea in 1950 and to blockade Cuba during the Cuban missile crisis of 1962, the author tests hypotheses about crisis decision making.

135   Hollick, Ann L., and Osgood, Robert E. NEW ERA OF OCEAN POLITICS. Baltimore: Johns Hopkins University Press, 1974. 131 p.

>   An examination of basic issues, major national and transnational interests, and processes by which international negotiations and national policymaking on ocean issues take place, with special emphasis on the United States.

136   Ikle, Fred Charles. HOW NATIONS NEGOTIATE. New York: Harper and Row, 1964. 274 p.

>   In an examination of negotiation as a science, the author sets forth general objectives of negotiation; considers the nature of bargaining from positions of strength and from weakness; sets forth rules of accommodation; and describes how negotiating parties come to terms. Included is an evaluation of the effectiveness, respectively, of the United States and the Soviet Union in international negotiations.

Foreign Policy and Diplomacy

137 Jacobson, Harold Karan, and Zimmerman, William, eds. THE SHAPING OF FOREIGN POLICY. New York: Atherton Press, 1969. 214 p.

An anthology containing essays illustrative of recent efforts to develop a comparative study of foreign policy. Included are writings dealing with systemic variables and models; environmental factors; structure and foreign policy; national images and international systems; and assumptions of rationality and nonrationality in models of the international system.

138 Johnson, E.A., ed. THE DIMENSIONS OF DIPLOMACY. Baltimore: Johns Hopkins University Press, 1964. 135 p.

An evaluation of the role of diplomacy in the context of the early 1960s. Included are essays on such topics as new techniques in diplomacy; the planning of foreign policy; power and diplomacy; and the assessments of several leading scholars and practitioners as to the adequacy of diplomacy for the needs of the twentieth-century world.

139 Kegley, Charles W., Jr., et al., eds. INTERNATIONAL EVENTS AND THE COMPARATIVE ANALYSIS OF FOREIGN POLICY. Columbia: University of South Carolina Press, 1975. 317 p.

A volume containing nine essays, including four published for the first time, on methodology, indicators of foreign policy behavior, and the results of empirical research on the comparative study of foreign policy. Focusing on the use of events data, the contributors address themselves to problems of measurement, conception, reliability and validity; comparative analysis and nomological explanation; and prediction, behavioral forecasts, and policymaking.

140 Kennan, George F. AMERICAN DIPLOMACY, 1900-1950. New York: Mentor Books, 1951. 144 p.

A good analysis of U.S. foreign policy with special emphasis on the Spanish-American War, the "Open Door" Policy in China, World War I, World War II, Soviet-American relations, together with an assessment of the nature of diplomacy in the modern world. The author examines the strengths and weaknesses of twentieth-century American diplomacy, and presents a framework for evaluation based on political realism.

141 Kissinger, Henry A. AMERICAN FOREIGN POLICY. Enl. ed. New York: W.W. Norton and Co., 1974. 304 p.

In addition to excellent essays on the domestic structure and foreign policy, the central issues of American foreign policy, and the Vietnam negotiations published in an earlier edition, (1972), this revised volume contains the text of speeches by

Foreign Policy and Diplomacy

the secretary of state on SALT and U.S.-Soviet relations; the "year of Europe"; the nature of the national dialogue on foreign policy; European unity and the Atlantic Community; and the quest for peace in the Middle East.

142 Lall, Arthur. MODERN INTERNATIONAL NEGOTIATION: PRINCIPLES AND PRACTICE. New York: Columbia University Press, 1966. 404 p.

An examination of the nature of international negotiations, with emphasis on the period since 1954, based to a large extent on the author's experience. Included are analyses of the role of third party intermediaries in mediation, conciliation, and good offices; factors that impede negotiation; the role of deterrence; and the function of international organizations in the resolution of conflicts among nations.

143 Levin, M. Gordon, Jr. WOODROW WILSON AND WORLD POLITICS. New York: Oxford University Press, 1968. 340 p.

An analysis of Wilson's theory of international relations and its application to American foreign policy between 1917 and 1919. Tracing American foreign policy from the Bolshevik Revolution through the U.S. intervention in Siberia, the author examines Wilson's efforts to assist Russian forces fighting the Bolsheviks to establish a liberal-nationalist regime. Extensive treatment is given to Wilson's attempts to moderate excessive allied demands against the defeated Central Powers in Europe and to dampen Japan's imperialistic ambitions in Asia.

144 Lovell, John P. FOREIGN POLICY IN PERSPECTIVE: STRATEGY, ADAPTATION, DECISION-MAKING. New York: Holt, Rinehart and Winston, 1970. 370 p.

An examination of American foreign policy based on a broad conceptual framework that includes hypotheses about the international system and the conduct of foreign policy. Drawn from theoretical literature and from the history of American involvement in world affairs, propositions are expounded on foreign policy strategies and tactics, the process and structure of foreign policy decision making, the goals and means of foreign policy, and the problem of reconciling demands for efficiency with the maintenance of democratic values.

145 McGowan, Patrick J., ed. SAGE INTERNATIONAL YEARBOOK OF FOREIGN POLICY STUDIES. Vol. I. Beverly Hills, Calif.: Sage Publications, 1973. 336 p.

A collection of ten writings representative of the research in the early 1970s which was designed to advance the comparative study of foreign policy. Included are chapters on such topics as scope and methods of foreign policy studies; simulation and theory building on foreign policy; public opinion and foreign policy; defense spending and senatorial voting behavior; and national attributes and foreign policy participation.

146 _____, ed. SAGE INTERNATIONAL YEARBOOK OF FOREIGN POLICY STUDIES. Vol. 2. Beverly Hills, Calif.: Sage Publications, 1974. 351 p.

> A second volume of nine writings based on recent research and theory-building efforts in comparative foreign policy studies. Included are chapters on adaptive behavior of small states, behavioral indicators of war proneness in bilateral conflicts, Bayesian analysis and the study of foreign policy behavior, and a bibliography of recent foreign policy studies.

147 Macomber, William. THE ANGELS' GAME: A HANDBOOK OF MODERN DIPLOMACY. New York: Stein and Day, 1975. 225 p.

> An analysis by an American diplomat of the qualities and skills essential to the effective conduct of diplomacy in a changing world. The author compares and contrasts contemporary and older diplomacy; discusses the diplomat as messenger-reporter; describes the art of negotiation; assesses relationships between diplomats and the Congress; and considers the role of the diplomat in the making of foreign policy.

148 Modelski, George. A THEORY OF FOREIGN POLICY. New York: Frederick A. Praeger, 1962. 152 p.

> Developing an input-output model, the author examines the processes by which foreign policy is formulated and put into operation. He analyzes propositions on the relationship between interests and objectives, interests and power, and internal and external factors and constraints.

149 Morgenthau, Hans J. THE IMPASSE OF AMERICAN FOREIGN POLICY. Chicago: University of Chicago Press, 1962. 312 p.

> The second of three volumes (see also Nos. 41 and 152) containing writings already published elsewhere by Professor Morgenthau. Included are selections on the foreign policies of the United States, the Soviet Union, the German Federal Republic, and Afro-Asian countries, as well as analyses of the United Nations and its political limitations.

150 _____. IN DEFENSE OF THE NATIONAL INTEREST: A CRITICAL EXAMINATION OF AMERICAN FOREIGN POLICY. New York: Alfred A. Knopf, 1951. 283 p.

> A critique of American foreign policy based on the author's conceptualization of national interest. The volume contains

analyses of utopianism, the nature of power, the role of diplomacy, and the mainsprings of American foreign policy in historical context and in the period following World War II.

151 _____. THE PURPOSE OF AMERICAN POLITICS. New York: Alfred A. Knopf, 1952. 359 p.

This mid-century study of the question of national purpose in the United States is based on historical analysis of evolving American goals in domestic policy and in foreign affairs. The author deals with the dilemmas faced by the United States in adapting its traditional purpose--the expansion of "equality in freedom"--to a world of great complexity. Throughout the study, an effort is made to relate the basic values and the political structure of the United States to the conduct of foreign policy.

152 _____. THE RESTORATION OF AMERICAN POLITICS. Chicago: University of Chicago Press, 1962. 391 p.

The third and final volume (see Nos. 41 and 149) in a series based on his published writings entitled "Politics in the Twentieth Century," in which the author explores the nature of politics in the nuclear age. Included are essays on such topics as the corruption of liberal thought; the decline of democratic government; deterrence theory; disarmament; alliances; diplomacy; the United Nations; and American foreign policy in Europe and Asia.

153 Needler, Martin C. UNDERSTANDING FOREIGN POLICY. New York: Holt, Rinehart and Winston, 1966. 280 p.

A short survey of the evolution of American foreign policy since World War II. Included are analyses of the nature of national interest in theory and practice; the formation of foreign policy in a democratic society; foreign policy machinery; the nature of the international system; the origins of the cold war; zones of international confrontation in Europe, Asia, and Latin America; and the prospects for American foreign policy.

154 Nicolson, Harold. DIPLOMACY. 2d ed. London: Oxford University Press, 1958. 248 p.

A concise, lucid survey of the evolution of diplomacy and diplomatic theory, the transition from older forms of diplomacy as practiced in the European state system to the modern diplomatic practices of the twentieth century, the nature of democratic diplomacy, types of European diplomacy, diplomatic procedure and language, and the evolution of the foreign service. This volume, written by a leading British diplomatist and writer, is of value both to the student and practitioner of diplomacy.

Foreign Policy and Diplomacy

155 Niebuhr, Reinhold. THE IRONY OF AMERICAN HISTORY. New York: Charles Scribner's Sons, 1952. 174 p.

   Niebuhr, a leading twentieth-century theologian, analyzes the values that have shaped both the American view of U.S. foreign policy and the role of the United States in world affairs. The author contends that such values, formed by the historic domestic experience of the United States, are not always relevant to resolving the complex problems facing American policymakers at the international level in the mid-twentieth century.

156 O'Leary, Michael K., and Coplin, William D. QUANTITATIVE TECHNIQUES IN FOREIGN POLICY ANALYSIS AND FORECASTING. New York: Frederick A. Praeger, 1975. 291 p.

   Based on collaboration between the Department of State and outside scholars, this volume embodies a study of the applicability of quantitative methods for foreign policy decision makers. In addition to surveying the current use of social science techniques in foreign affairs analysis, the authors present six case studies employing quantitative methodologies on topics such as elections abroad; military expenditures in Latin America; international bargaining; projections of violence; and coalition behavior in global oil politics.

157 Organski, A.F.K. WORLD POLITICS. New York: Alfred A. Knopf, 1961. 461 p.

   A textbook based on a framework in which the nation and its foreign policy capabilities and goals are examined; the nature and determinants of national power are considered; and the role of collective security and international organizations is assessed. The volume includes a detailed critique of realist theory and the balance of power, as well as chapters devoted to colonialism, diplomacy, geography, resources, and population.

158 Osgood, Robert E. IDEALS AND SELF-INTEREST IN AMERICA'S FOREIGN RELATIONS: THE GREAT TRANSFORMATION OF THE TWENTIETH CENTURY. Chicago: University of Chicago Press, 1953. 491 p.

   A highly useful examination of the evolution of American attitudes toward world affairs since the beginning of the twentieth century with emphasis on universal ideals and national self-interest as guiding principles. Included is an analysis of the part that such principles have actually played, what Americans have considered their role to be, and the author's conception of the place, respectively, of universal ideals and self-interest in mid-twentieth-century American foreign policy.

Foreign Policy and Diplomacy

159 Paige, Glenn D. THE KOREAN DECISION: JUNE 24-30, 1950. New York: Free Press, 1968. 394 p.

    Testing propositions from decision-making theories, the author reconstructs and analyzes the U.S. decision to assist the Republic of Korea to defend itself against the invasion from North Korea. He identifies major variables, including time available for decision making, the internal and external setting, the decisional unit, bureaucratic roles, and communications among decision makers under crisis situations.

160 Rosenau, James N. NATIONAL LEADERSHIP AND FOREIGN POLICY: A CASE STUDY IN THE MOBILIZATION OF PUBLIC SUPPORT. Princeton, N.J.: Princeton University Press, 1963. 409 p.

    An examination of the structure of American national leadership in the private sector and its function in the formation of a consensus about American foreign policy. Basing his study on data derived from a questionnaire distributed to attendees of a White House Conference on foreign aid in 1957, the author compares social backgrounds, political behavior, and opinion-making activities of a cross-section of corporate executives, labor leaders, educators, and heads of voluntary organizations.

161 _____. THE SCIENTIFIC STUDY OF FOREIGN POLICY. New York: Free Press, 1972. 472 p.

    A collection of the author's published writings on conceptual and methodological problems of foreign policy research. Included are essays on the behavioral study of international relations, the nature of systematic and comparative analysis, foreign policy as an issue-area, the study of domestic-international linkages, the concept of national interest, and intervention as a scientific concept.

162 _____, ed. COMPARING FOREIGN POLICIES: THEORIES, FINDINGS, AND METHODS. New York: Halsted Press Division, John Wiley and Sons, 1974; Sage Publications. 442 p.

    A volume containing seventeen essays representing the results of pioneering research conducted by the Inter-University Comparative Foreign Policy project. Among the topics examined are foreign policy behavior in dyadic relationships; a causal modeling approach; governmental and societal influences on foreign policy in open and closed nations; leader personality; national, systemic, and external attributes in foreign policy analysis; problems of events data reliability; and the relationship between internation conflict resolution and national attributes.

Foreign Policy and Diplomacy

163 _____, ed. DOMESTIC SOURCES OF FOREIGN POLICY. New York: Free Press, 1967. 340 p.

> A series of important essays dealing with foreign policy as an issue area; personality and attitude correlates in foreign policy; the relationship between social position, party identification and foreign policy; mass communications, interest groups, voting behavior and foreign policy.

164 _____, ed. LINKAGE POLITICS: ESSAYS ON THE CONVERGENCE OF NATIONAL AND INTERNATIONAL SYSTEMS. New York: Free Press, 1969. 352 p.

> An impressive attempt to develop conceptual frameworks and methodologies for the exploration of the flow of influence between the international system and national systems. Several scholars examine the nature of national-international linkages in superpowers, major powers, and less developed countries.

165 Rourke, Francis E. BUREAUCRACY AND FOREIGN POLICY. Baltimore: Johns Hopkins University Press, 1972. 80 p.

> An examination of bureaucratic factors and their influence on the shaping of foreign policy. The author assesses the role, existing and potential, as well as the capabilities and limitations of bureaucracies in the formation of foreign policy, with special emphasis on the United States.

166 Rummel, R.J. DIMENSIONS OF NATIONS. Beverly Hills, Calif.: Sage Publications, 1972. 512 p.

> A volume containing research strategy and findings from a large-scale project designed to compare nations by the analysis of data on such characteristics and dimensions as economic development, size, density of population, and voting patterns in international organizations. Utilizing factor analysis, the author develops correlations about domestic and international conflict behavior and other aspects of the foreign policy of nations.

167 Satow, Ernest. A GUIDE TO DIPLOMATIC PRACTICE. 2 vols. London: Longmans, Green and Co., 1922. Vol. 1, 419 p.; vol. 2, 438 p.

> An extensive treatise on the nature of diplomacy and the duties of the diplomatist, as well as the rules guiding diplomatic behavior. Included are chapters on such topics as the language of diplomatic discourse; the right of legation; diplomatic immunities; extra-territoriality; termination of a mission; treaties and other international agreements; and diplomatic procedures at congresses and conferences.

168 Schou, August, and Olau, Arne, eds. SMALL STATES IN INTERNATIONAL RELATIONS. Nobel Symposium 17. New York: Wiley Interscience Division, John Wiley and Sons, 1971. 250 p.

> An international group of nineteen scholars address themselves to the foreign policies of small states, with emphasis on such topics as an analysis of small power politics; nonalignment and alliance systems; permanent neutrality; small states and international peacekeeping; and the impact of nuclear weapons on the foreign policies of small states.

169 Snyder, Richard C., et al., eds. FOREIGN POLICY DECISION-MAKING: AN APPROACH TO THE STUDY OF INTERNATIONAL POLITICS. New York: Free Press of Glencoe, 1962. 274 p.

> An important volume containing a decision-making framework representing one of the early efforts to develop a comparative study of foreign policy and provide the basis for "middle range" theories of international relations. Included is an application of the model to the decision of the United States in June 1950 to resist aggression in Korea, as well as chapters evaluating strategies and conceptual schemes for the study of international relations.

170 Thayer, Charles W. DIPLOMAT. New York: Harper and Brothers, 1959. 299 p.

> An examination of the nature, methods, and mechanics of diplomacy in various contexts, older and contemporary, totalitarian and democratic. The author, a diplomatist, describes the operation of an embassy; the conduct of Soviet and American diplomacy; diplomatic privileges and immunities; and diplomacy and intelligence.

171 Vital, David. THE SURVIVAL OF SMALL STATES: STUDIES IN SMALL POWER-GREAT POWER CONFLICT. London: Oxford University Press, 1971. 136 p.

> After developing a model for the study of relations between small states and great powers, the author examines the foreign policy of three small states: Czechoslovakia at the time of the 1938 Munich crisis; Israel's relations with the United States and the Soviet Union; and the problems for Finland's independence posed by the Soviet Union. Included are analyses of the foreign policies and options available to small powers.

172 Webster, Charles. THE ART AND PRACTICE OF DIPLOMACY. New York: Barnes and Noble, 1962. 246 p.

> An examination of diplomacy based largely on the British experience of the nineteenth and twentieth centuries. Included

are chapters on the machinery of British foreign policy; changes in teaching and research on diplomacy; and principal British statesmen and diplomatists.

173 Wilkinson, David O. COMPARATIVE FOREIGN RELATIONS: FRAMEWORK AND METHODS. Belmont, Calif.: Dickenson Publishing Co., 1969. 191 p.

> The author sets forth a framework for the comparative analysis of foreign policies, based on such factors as perceived national roles; the spectrum of capabilities; the nature of will; political institutions and processes; and leadership. Included is an examination of problems in analyzing current foreign policy and developing forecasts in order to anticipate future trends.

174 Wirsing, Robert G., ed. INTERNATIONAL RELATIONS AND THE FUTURE OF OCEAN SPACE. Columbia: University of South Carolina Press, 1974. 146 p.

> In original essays five contributors address themselves to problems of ocean resources, especially as they impinge on U.S. foreign policy. Included are analyses of problems of the Law of the Sea Conference; special domestic interests and U.S. oceans policy; and approaches to the control of ocean pollution and resources.

Chapter 5
POWER AND INTERNATIONAL RELATIONS

Some writers have held that all political relationships are power relationships. In the words of Hans Morgenthau, "All politics is a struggle for power" defined in terms of national interest.[1] Others, like E.H. Carr, have observed that "while politics cannot be satisfactorily defined exclusively in terms of power, it is safe to say that power is always an essential element of politics."[2] States take as a principal task the preservation of their interests against the competing interests of other states.

Although power has been a focal point for the study of international relations, it has had widely differing meanings to scholars of international relations. While realist writers sought to categorize and study the elements of power, a more recent generation of scholars has made an effort to measure power more precisely and to determine empirically the role of power in foreign policy decision making and in international relations. Despite the lack of consensus among international relations scholars about the meaning of power, there is agreement that power connotes something more than the ability to coerce by force and thus includes more than military capabilities. While the centrality of power posited by some scholars, notably realists, is disputed by others, power as a concept has been studied extensively in the literature of international relations.

In general, scholars of international relations identify power as a capacity for influencing the behavior of other nations, groups, or individuals in some desired fashion by means of persuasion, leadership, threats, promises, or force. The effective exercise of power in international relations, it is usually suggested, depends upon the quality--and quantity--of such factors as leadership, population, morale, natural resources, science and technology, economic development, and military capabilities. According to some writers--proponents of geopolitical analysis--the power of nations has been affected by such geographic factors as

---

[1] Hans J. Morgenthau, POLITICS AMONG NATIONS (No. 106), p. 5.

[2] E.H. Carr, THE TWENTY YEARS' CRISIS (No. 8), p. 102. See also Nos. 191, 194, 201, and 203.

secure frontiers, access to the oceans, internal communications, and natural resource endowment.

International relations scholars, as well as policymakers, have placed great emphasis on study of the factors of power, or the analysis of the relative capabilities of nations to each other. An understanding of the capabilities of nations, as well as the intentions of policymakers, is crucial to the policymaker and is the object of analysis by the scholar. Decision makers engage in a continuing comparison and analysis of their own national capabilities, as well as those of other nations. Whatever the problems of discerning with accuracy capabilities, it is even more difficult to assess with precision the intentions of the decision makers of other nations. Capabilities are useful, but not always reliable, indicators of intentions. In addition, national capabilities are relative and always subject to change. As the nature of the international system changes, so does the relative importance of each national capability, even if the capability itself remains constant.

Closely related to power as a focal point for analysis is the concept of balance of power. Much of the literature on power is addressed also to balance of power both in theory and practice.[3] Like power itself, the concept of balance of power has been defined in many ways and used by scholars to mean quite different things. Balance of power has been used to denote an equilibrium of power among nations; it also has been used simply to describe a distribution of power. In practice, too, difficulties with the balance of power concept have arisen. For instance, statesmen have not always enjoyed the political flexibility in foreign affairs that is demanded by balance of power theory, namely, a capacity to shift from alignment with one country to another in response to changing national interests and threats to security.

The concept of balance of power has been subject to close scrutiny in the international relations literature of the past generation. Balance of power has been used in models of international systems developed by scholars. Efforts have been made to study and compare the balance of power in contrasting international systems of the past. Theories of balance of power have been tested by use of historical materials. Scholars have concerned themselves with the balance of power and the management of power in a variety of conceptual models of international systems, such as bipolar and multipolar. The development of a world containing additional power centers--noted by scholars and practitioners alike to be characteristic of the 1970s--has spurred an interest in balance of power and the relevance of theories of power balance to the study and stability of the emerging international system. In an international system based on autonomous units, power and its management, and the balance, or distribution, of power are important elements that influence national foreign policies. Thus, discussion of the nature and scope of power held by nations and other actors will in all likelihood remain important in the study of international relations.

---

[3]See, for example, Nos. 179 and 189.

175 Berle, Adolf A. POWER. New York: Harcourt, Brace and World, 1969. 603 p.

>   An assessment of the concept of power and its manifestation within and among nations, at the interpersonal and international levels. The author examines the role of institutions, the nature of economic power, the major theories and elements of international power, and the limitations of balance of power and international organization in managing power relationships among nations.

176 Brucan, Silviu. THE DISSOLUTION OF POWER: THE SOCIOLOGY OF INTERNATIONAL RELATIONS AND POLITICS. New York: Alfred A. Knopf, 1971. 388 p.

>   An analysis of major forces shaping the world of the late twentieth century with special emphasis on nationalism, technology, and the nature of power, conflict, and revolution. The author examines forces making for integration and disintegration, and sets forth his conception of the emerging global system.

177 Brzezinski, Zbigniew. BETWEEN TWO AGES: AMERICA'S ROLE IN THE TECHNETRONIC ERA. New York: Viking Press, 1970. 334 p.

>   A perceptive and important analysis of the impact of the scientific-technological revolution on international relations and the transition of the United States, as the most advanced industrial society, to a new "technetronic" era. In addition to his extensive examination of emerging political, social, and economic patterns in the United States, the author assesses the implications of the global technological revolution for communist states and the less developed nations.

178 Buchan, Alastair. POWER AND EQUILIBRIUM IN THE 1970'S. New York: Frederick A. Praeger for the Council on Foreign Relations, 1973. 120 p.

>   This study, based on a series of lectures presented under the auspices of the Council on Foreign Relations, is devoted to an analysis of the nature of bipolarity-multipolarity in the contemprary world. The author examines the nature of the historical balance of power and develops a model for the present international system based on four principal types of power--strategic capabilities, conventional military strength, political influence, and economic power. Of central concern is the manner in which power is being redistributed among existing major actors and to new power centers in the world of the 1970s.

179 Claude, Inis L., Jr. POWER AND INTERNATIONAL RELATIONS. New York: Random House, 1962. 310 p.

>   Reviewing the extensive literature on balance of power, collec-

tive security, and world government as frameworks for the management of power. The author evaluates the utility and limitations of these frameworks in the contemporary world through analyses and critiques of the assumptions, meanings, and applications of each for power management at the international level. An extensive bibliography is included.

180   Cohen, Saul B.   GEOGRAPHY AND POLITICS IN A WORLD DIVIDED. New York: Random House, 1963.   347 p.

A review and critique of ancient and recent literature on the role of land power and sea power in geopolitical relationships, as well as an assessment of the relationship between geography and power in the post World War II international system. Focusing on each of the regions, the author describes the power centers in a divided world, and presents his own geopolitical analysis, including distribution of population and resources and location vis-à-vis other power centers.

181   Cox, Kevin R., et al., eds.   LOCATIONAL APPROACHES TO POWER AND CONFLICT.   New York: Halsted Press Division, John Wiley and Sons, 1974.   345 p.

A collection of eleven original essays whose authors assess the meaning of boundaries and territory, politics and geography, in the study and analysis of international relations. Among the topics examined are locational aspects of political integration; the geographical analysis of political systems; and territorial organization and conflict.

182   DeJouvenel, Bertrand.   ON POWER: ITS NATURE AND THE HISTORY OF ITS GROWTH.   Boston: Beacon Press, 1962.   421 p.

A major treatise on the origins and historical manifestations of power from the ancient world to modern times. The author assesses the nature of civil disobedience, revolution, and totalitarianism; theories of sovereignty; organic theories of power; power and law; and the role of beliefs in sustaining or limiting power.

183   De la Blache, Vidal.   PRINCIPLES OF HUMAN GEOGRAPHY.   New York: Henry Holt and Co., 1926.   511 p.

A volume synthesizing the earlier writings of the founder of the modern French school of geography in which the author surveys human geography from ancient civilizations to the early twentieth century. Included is a critical examination of the meaning of human geography, as well as the growth of population density in Africa, Asia, and Europe; the evolution of transportation and communications networks and patterns; and the location of raw materials and the development of tools for the exploitation of the environment.

184 Dorpalen, Andreas. THE WORLD OF GENERAL HAUSHOFER: GEOPOLITICS IN ACTION. New York: Farrar and Rinehart, 1942. 337 p.

> The author traces the evolution of geopolitical theory and analyzes in detail the writings of Karl Haushofer. The volume contains an examination of geopolitics and economic policy, and war and population policy, as well as selections from the writings of major theorists of geopolitics.

185 Emeny, Brooks. THE STRATEGY OF RAW MATERIALS: A STUDY OF AMERICA IN PEACE AND WAR. New York: Macmillan Co., 1934. 202 p.

> An early analysis of the role of raw materials and foodstuffs in the power potential of nations, with special reference to the United States in the interwar period. The author surveys world resources and their distribution in minerals, metals, and agricultural production.

186 Fairgrieve, James. GEOGRAPHY AND WORLD POWER. London: University of London Press, 1948. 376 p.

> The author assesses the impact of geography on the development of civilizations from ancient Egypt to the modern period. Among the topics examined are patterns of migration; mobility over land and sea; natural barriers to, and avenues for, the movement of population; the distribution of natural resources; and climatic factors as they have influenced the global system.

187 Ferkiss, Victor. THE FUTURE OF TECHNOLOGICAL CIVILIZATION. New York: George Braziller, 1974. 369 p.

> This critique of major conservative and liberal theories and existing frameworks for political organization is based on an examination of the impact of science and technology on society. After setting forth a conception of the emerging world of the future, the author calls for the development of a new ecological humanism.

188 Finkelstein, Marina S., and Finkelstein, Lawrence S., eds. COLLECTIVE SECURITY. San Francisco: Chandler Publishing Co., 1966. 278 p.

> An anthology of 110 writings dealing with the theory and practice of collective security in historical and contemporary contexts. Among the topics examined are the relationship between balance of power and collective security; the problems of collective security in the nuclear age; and the prerequisites for the successful operation of collective security.

189 Gulick, Edward V. EUROPE'S CLASSICAL BALANCE OF POWER. Ithaca, N.Y.: Cornell University Press, 1955. 337 p.

Drawing upon the extensive literature about balance of power, the author develops a balance of power framework which he then utilizes in analyzing the period preceding the Congress of Vienna (1812-15) and leading to the Concert of Europe. Included is an analysis of the nature, assumptions, means, and goals of the balance of power.

190 Hauser, Philip M., ed. POPULATION AND WORLD POLITICS. Glencoe, Ill.: Free Press, 1958. 297 p.

A collection of twelve original essays on the implications of population for international politics. The authors address such problems as the effects of population trends on natural resources; patterns of international migration; population as a factor in economic development; population and political instability; and population and American foreign policy.

191 Knorr, Klaus. POWER AND WEALTH: THE POLITICAL ECONOMY OF INTERNATIONAL POWER. New York: Basic Books, 1973. 210 p.

An examination of how nations acquire resources and develop and make use of power. The author analyzes the nature of power and influence; foreign policy and national interest; and the foundations and uses of military and economic power.

192 Mackinder, Sir Halford J. DEMOCRATIC IDEALS AND REALITY. 1919. Reprint. New York: W.W. Norton and Co., 1962. 278 p.

A classic work on geography and world power in which the author sets forth his famous theory that control of the Eurasian "heartland" (Central and Eastern Europe) is the key to global supremacy. In this volume, Mackinder traces the evolution of land powers and sea powers since ancient times and concludes that the great land powers usually become dominant both on land and on the seas.

193 Mahan, Alfred Thayer. THE INFLUENCE OF SEA POWER UPON HISTORY, 1660-1783. 2d ed. London: Methuen and Co., 1964. 557 p.

A classic and important study of Britain's rise to preeminence through the development of sea power and naval victories over European rivals. The author presents a detailed analysis of the elements of sea power based on a vivid description of major naval battles between 1660 and 1783.

194 Morgenstern, Oskar, et al. LONG TERM PROJECTIONS OF POWER: POLITICAL, ECONOMIC, AND MILITARY FORECASTING. Cambridge, Mass.: Ballinger Publishing Co., 1973. 229 p.

A critique of forecasting techniques including quantitative-analytical approaches, simulation, and time-series analysis with emphasis on technological change and the power potential of the United States, the Soviet Union, China, Japan, and Western Europe. The authors examine the content of future technology and the energy crisis, and present a series of conclusions on the uses and limitations of forecasting.

195 Morgenthau, Hans J. SCIENTIFIC MAN VS. POWER POLITICS. Chicago: University of Chicago Press, 1952. 245 p.

An attempt to assess the sources of the widespread inability of democracies allegedly to respond effectively to the international challenges that culminated in World War II. The author presents a trenchant critique of the notion that international political problems, like those of the natural sciences, can be resolved through increased understanding and education of the parties to the conflict since, according to Morgenthau, disputes among nations derive from competition for power rather than misconceptions of the issues at stake.

196 Nagel, Jack. THE DESCRIPTIVE ANALYSIS OF POWER. New Haven and London: Yale University Press, 1975. 200 p.

An effort to define power as a causal relationship and to develop new techniques for the measurement of power by means of the statistical technique of path analysis. Included are analyses of causation, indirect influence, symmetry and asymmetry in power relations, and the relationship between power and conflict.

197 Organski, Katherine, and Organski, A.F.K. POPULATION AND WORLD POWER. New York: Alfred A. Knopf, 1961. 263 p.

An analysis of the relationship between population and national power. Among the topics examined are the population explosion; national population policies; international integration; and problems for political development posed by population growth.

198 Schuman, Frederick L. THE COMMONWEALTH OF MAN: AN INQUIRY INTO POWER POLITICS AND WORLD GOVERNMENT. New York: Alfred A. Knopf, 1952. 494 p.

Tracing historical efforts to achieve global unity, the author attributes to the existence of sovereign nation-states the world disorder of the twentieth century. He proposes the formation of a global federation in order to reduce the risk of international conflict and to cope with other problems whose solution lies beyond the grasp of the nation-state.

199 Singer, Marshall R. WEAK STATES IN A WORLD OF POWERS: THE DYNAMICS OF INTERNATIONAL RELATIONSHIPS. New York: Free Press, 1972. 431 p.

After an analysis and critique of power as a concept, the author explores existing relationships between weak and powerful states, drawing on data collected on 130 countries. Included is a model based on perceptions, communications, dependence, and independence. Among the power relationships examined are political, economic, and military ties. The volume contains policy recommendations for weak and strong states in their relations with each other.

200 Sprout, Harold, and Sprout, Margaret. THE ECOLOGICAL PERSPECTIVE ON HUMAN AFFAIRS WITH SPECIAL REFERENCE TO INTERNATIONAL POLITICS. Princeton, N.J.: Princeton University Press, 1965. 236 p.

A critical survey of much of the literature dealing with geography and other environmental factors as determinants of international behavior. Major attention is devoted to schools of thought characterized by the authors as environmental determinism, free-will environmentalism, and possibilism. Included is an examination of the cognitive and predictive aspects of man-milieu relationships, together with the authors' own framework for analysis purporting to show the central importance of the "ecological approach" in all approaches to the study of international politics.

201 Spykman, Nicholas J. AMERICA'S STRATEGY IN WORLD POLITICS: THE UNITED STATES AND THE BALANCE OF POWER. New York: Harcourt, Brace and Co., 1942. 500 p.

An important analysis of the nature of power within a geopolitical framework, with emphasis on American foreign policy and the isolationist-internationalist debate on the eve of U.S. entry into World War II. The author examines U.S. interests in Europe, Asia, and the Western Hemisphere, and sets forth his conception of the shape of the postwar world and the need, as he saw it, for the restoration of a balance of power.

202 _____. THE GEOGRAPHY OF THE PEACE. New York: Harcourt, Brace and Co., 1944. 66 p.

A geopolitical analysis of the international system and of American national security interests in the period following World War II. The author examines the conditioning factors of foreign policy; older conceptions of the Heartland and Rimland; strategic patterns of World War II; and Eurasian conflict zones.

203 Strausz-Hupé, Robert. THE BALANCE OF TOMORROW: POWER AND FOREIGN POLICY IN THE UNITED STATES. New York: G.P. Putnam's Sons, 1945. 302 p.

A detailed examination of the nature of power in international relations with special emphasis on population, raw materials, industrialization, and technology. Included are demographic analyses of world powers and the distribution of resources, together with the author's assessment of the capabilities, existing and potential, of the United States and other countries.

204 _____. GEOPOLITICS: THE STRUGGLE FOR SPACE AND POWER. New York: G.P. Putnam's Sons 1942. 274 p.

An excellent examination of the evolution of geopolitical thought in early twentieth-century Germany, which focuses on the work of Karl Haushofer between the two world wars. The volume contains an extended treatment and critique of geopolitical conceptions of the heartland; doctrines of land power and sea power; and geographical patterns of history.

205 Weigert, Hans W. GENERALS AND GEOGRAPHERS: THE TWILIGHT OF GEOPOLITICS. New York: Oxford University Press, 1942. 273 p.

An examination of major schools of geopolitical analysis of the early twentieth century. The author places emphasis on the writings of Mackinder and Haushofer, as well as the implications of geopolitical theory for American foreign policy and strategy in World War II.

206 Winslow, E.M. THE PATTERN OF IMPERIALISM: A STUDY IN THE THEORIES OF POWER. New York: Columbia University Press, 1948. 278 p.

An analysis and critique of writings on imperialism with focus on economic theories. The author examines the ideas of Adam Smith and John Hobson, anti-imperialism in the United States, Marxian theories of imperialism and Lenin's writings, and the limitations of economic interpretations in understanding the nature of imperialism.

Chapter 6
MILITARY STRATEGY AND THEORIES OF DETERRENCE

In pursuit of their national interests, states historically have come into conflict. Thus, military capabilities and strategies form a crucial element of a nation's power. Although military strategy and the development of strategic theories have always been of major concern to international relations scholars, since World War II the study of national security policies has become a major area of interest in international relations. The vast increase in destructive potential resulting from the development of nuclear weapons, together with the propensity toward conflict in the world of the last thirty years, has led increasing numbers of scholars and policy analysts, within universities and research organizations, to study international security problems. A subfield in the study of international relations has been developed, with emphasis being placed on such phenomena as deterrence theory, limited war, unconventional conflict, theories of escalation, arms control and disarmament, defense decision making, and the implications of new technologies for the conduct of warfare.

Scholars and policy analysts have sought to understand the role of force in the achievement of foreign policy goals. The greatest emphasis, however, of international security studies has been the development of theories of nuclear deterrence and arms control. While the problem of deterrence had been of interest to theorists before the nuclear age, there has been a major effort over the past generation to refine theories of deterrence and to develop theoretical analyses having policy implications. The destructive potential of nuclear weapons, together with their possession by both the United States and the Soviet Union, gave impetus to analyses of the conditions for deterring conflict and achieving greater stability in superpower nuclear relationships.

Underlying deterrence theory are several implicit assumptions that are revealed in much of the literature of strategic studies. The most pervasive assumption of deterrence theory suggests that the level of destruction that would result from a nuclear conflict by far outweighs the value of the objective sought. By and large, deterrence theorists have assumed that nations will only deploy their nuclear weapons when vital national interests are at stake. For example, some analysts have hypothesized that in a nuclear age a nation's security must be based on possession of national atomic capabilities, rather than reliance on the nuclear guarantees of allies. The quest for the answer to questions about the credibility of superpower nuclear guarantees and the prerequisites for nuclear deterrence led, in the case of France, to the development of a national atomic force.[1] In the United States it has occasioned a continuing debate over the capabilities needed to maintain a deterrent relationship with the Soviet Union.[2]

Much of the discussion of strategic doctrine since World War II has taken place in a largely bipolar nuclear world. With the emergence of additional nuclear powers and the development by the Soviet Union of a military capability rivaling that of the United States, defense analysts have begun to focus attention on the concept of strategic parity and its implications for U.S.-Soviet relations, nuclear proliferation, and stability in the international system. The adequacy of existing deterrence theory in an international environment that is becoming less bipolar, and indeed will be increasingly multinuclear, is already the focus of interest in contemporary international security literature.[3]

Although the principal emphasis of writers on military strategy since World War II has been upon nuclear weapons and especially theories of deterrence, there has also been substantial interest in the study of conflict at other levels. In their efforts to understand the nature of limited war in the nuclear age, scholars have undertaken studies of wars over the last thirty years not only in order to describe such conflicts, but also to theorize about them and to develop doctrines for deterring conflict at the battlefield level. There is a substantial literature about nonnuclear conflict in the nuclear age as well as about the role of tactical nuclear weapons in deterring conflict, for example, in Central Europe. Closely related to such studies have been analyses of escalation, de-escalation and war termination. Strategic analysts have sought to understand more clearly the process by which conflicts escalate--for example from a limited war to a strategic exchange between the United States and the Soviet Union. In addition, the concern of writers with such phenomena as escalation, de-escalation, war termination, and deterrence has contributed to a growing interest in crisis management. Here, it should be noted, there is a close linkage between the study of conflict and the study of decision making. Much of the literature of decision making--discussed in Chapter 4 of this volume--has been focused on the decision-making process under conditions of international crisis.

---

[1] See, for example, Pierre Gallois, THE BALANCE OF TERROR (No. 223). Gallois first suggested this thesis that later became a prominent theme of President Charles de Gaulle's diplomacy.

[2] See, for example, Albert Wohlstetter, "The Delicate Balance of Terror," FOREIGN AFFAIRS, January 1959, pp. 211-34; William R. Van Cleave and Robert W. Barnett, "Strategic Adaptability," ORBIS, Fall 1974, pp. 655-76. See also Nos. 210, 216, 225, 229, 231, 236, 237, 241, 244, 247, and 262.

[3] See, for example, Fred C. Iklé, "Can Deterrence Last Out the Century," FOREIGN AFFAIRS, January 1973, pp. 267-85. See also No. 240.

Military Strategy and Deterrence

The immense destructive potential of military capabilities has contributed to a growth in the study of arms control and disarmament. While such phenomena have long been of interest to students of international relations, a major new literature dealing with theoretical as well as practical aspects of disarmament and arms control has emerged since World War II. Problems of nuclear proliferation, the limitation of strategic armaments, the relationship between deterrence and the limitation of armaments, the problems of arms reduction, and limitation at the nonnuclear level have all been widely discussed in writings in this field.

Much of the conflict of the past thirty years has taken place at a level of relatively unsophisticated weaponry. Much of the so-called Third World has been in the throes of revolutionary change, much of it the aftermath of European empire. Such conflicts have taken place between contending factions within colonial territories and within new states. They have also led to intervention by outside powers--directly, as in the case of the United States in South Vietnam, and indirectly, as with the Soviet Union in North Vietnam. There has been a considerable emphasis in defense literature on the conduct of revolutionary warfare, drawing upon theories developed by practitioners such as Mao Tse-tung, Fidel Castro, and Che Guevara as well as by academic analysts. In addition an effort has been made to assess the relationship, if any, between the level of conflict within a country and its general propensity toward violence at the international level.

The persistence of conflict-laden problems within and among nations, the rise of new nonstate actors such as terrorist groups, and the development of ever more advanced weapons will assure a major place in the literature of international relations for the study of theoretical and practical aspects of conflict in the last quarter of the twentieth century. Scholars and policy analysts will seek answers to questions about the stability of deterrence in a multinuclear world, the limitation of conflict among nations and among dissident nonstate groups, and the conditions for the achievement of a more peaceful world.

207 Angell, Norman. THE GREAT ILLUSION: A STUDY OF THE RELATION OF MILITARY POWER TO NATIONAL ADVANTAGE. New York: G.P. Putnam's Sons, 1913. 416 p.

> An early twentieth-century critique of imperial expansion for economic gain in a period of increasing interdependence among nations. The author examines the assumption that national prosperity depends on military power; describes in detail the processes of international trade; and sets forth his conception of a changing world and the requirements for a peaceful international order.

208 Aron, Raymond. THE CENTURY OF TOTAL WAR. Garden City, N.Y.: Doubleday and Co., 1954. 379 p.

> This useful assessment of the changed role of warfare in the twentieth century is based on analyses of the two world wars,

as well as the development of new technologies, including nuclear weapons, and the emergence of the United States and the Soviet Union as principal powers. In addition to examining the impact of such factors as nationalism and technology on international politics, the author considers the nature of limited war, alliances, and international equilibrium in the context of cold war.

209 _____. ON WAR. New York: W.W. Norton & Co., 1968. 143 p.

This analysis of the evolution of warfare as an instrument of state policy focuses on both nuclear and nonnuclear conflict. The author contends that nuclear weapons have produced neither a peace made stable by fear nor a certain global catastrophe; they have merely altered conditions for the conduct of war and diplomacy, both of which he describes in this volume.

210 Beaufre, André. DETERRENCE AND STRATEGY. New York: Frederick A. Praeger, 1966. 174 p.

In an important work, the author develops a theory of deterrence in light of the levels of use of force--nuclear and non-nuclear--and number of participants. Included are the following: assessments of the problems of alliances in the nuclear age; the development of independent nuclear forces and the proliferation of nuclear weapons; and the implications of nuclear deterrence for strategy and for the conduct of national security policy.

211 Bennett, John C., ed. NUCLEAR WEAPONS AND THE CONFLICT OF CONSCIENCE. London: Butterworth Press, 1962. 191 p.

Seven scholars, including the editor, address themselves to ethical aspects of nuclear weapons and conflict. Included are chapters on the nature of nuclear war; the idea of unilateral disarmament; and the concept of "just war" in the atomic age.

212 Bobrow, Davis B., ed. COMPONENTS OF DEFENSE POLICY. Chicago: Rand McNally and Co., 1965. 445 p.

An anthology containing writings on the strategic-military policies of the Soviet Union and China; defense policymaking; deterrence theory; guerrilla war and counterinsurgency; civil defense; arms control and disarmament; rationality and nonrationality in models of the international system; and civil-military relations in the context of postwar American defense policy.

213 Boulding, Kenneth E. CONFLICT AND DEFENSE: A GENERAL THEORY. New York: Harper and Row, 1962. 349 p.

The author adapts economic models and theories of economics

to the study of international conflict and its resolution. Static and dynamic conflict models, together with game theory, are examined. Thus the "general theory" developed in this volume is based on the premise that all conflicts have common elements, general patterns, and social processes.

214 Brodie, Bernard. STRATEGY IN THE MISSILE AGE. Princeton, N.J.: Princeton University Press, 1965. 423 p.

A good examination of the evolution of air strategy before and during World War II and in the first postwar decade. The author assesses the role and effectiveness of strategic bombing in World War II, the anatomy of deterrence in the nuclear age, and the problems of limited war in a world of atomic superpowers.

215 _____. WAR AND POLITICS. New York: Macmillan Co., 1973. 514 p.

A study by an eminent authority of the relationship between strategy and politics, changing social attitudes toward war, and the nature of "vital interests" that have led nations to resort to war in major conflicts of the twentieth century--World War I, World War II, Korea, and Vietnam. A major portion of the volume is devoted to a consideration of nuclear weapons and deterrence theory.

216 Brodie, Bernard, and Brodie, Fawn M. FROM CROSSBOW TO H-BOMB: THE EVOLUTION OF THE WEAPONS AND TACTICS OF WARFARE. Bloomington: Indiana University Press, 1973. 320 p.

An historical analysis of the application of science to war from ancient times to the twentieth century. The volume contains chapters on such topics as the impact of gunpowder on the conduct of conflict; war and science between the seventeenth and nineteenth centuries; technological innovations in the two world wars; the strategic implications of the nuclear revolution; and the utilization of systems analysis in defense decision-making.

217 Brown, Neville. STRATEGIC MOBILITY. New York: Frederick A. Praeger, for the Institute for Strategic Studies, 1964. 254 p.

An analysis of the strategic capabilities needed for a defense based on the mobility of military forces. The author examines British and American experiences since World War II in deploying forces rapidly to conflict environments around the world. Among the topics treated are sea-based capabilities, mobility by air, the role of bases, and ground forces in limited war.

218 Bull, Hedley. THE CONTROL OF THE ARMS RACE: DISARMAMENT AND ARMS CONTROL IN THE MISSILE AGE. New York: Frederick A. Praeger, 1961. 215 p.

> A trenchant analysis of the objectives of, and essential conditions for, arms control and disarmament. The author examines the problems of nuclear and conventional disarmament; assesses the obstacles to general and complete disarmament; develops important conceptual distinctions between arms control and disarmament; and presents a critique of theories about the relationship between arms races and international conflict.

219 Collins, John M. GRAND STRATEGY: PRACTICES AND PRINCIPLES. Annapolis, Md.: Naval Institute Press, 1973. 338 p.

> A basic text designed to provide a concise compendium of strategic concepts and principles and an analysis of strategy in both a historical and contemporary context. The author examines the evolution of strategic thought; ends versus means relationships; the nature of threat assessment; principles of general war, limited war, and revolutionary war; concepts of deterrence; economic and fiscal constraints; science, technology and strategy; and U.S. defense policy in Europe, Asia, and the Middle East.

220 Debray, Régis. STRATEGY FOR REVOLUTION: ESSAYS ON LATIN AMERICA. New York: Monthly Review Press, 1969. 256 p.

> A collection of the writings of a theoretician and practitioner of revolution in Latin America. Included are the author's analyses of Castroism, his assessment of problems of revolutionary strategy in Latin America, and a report of his own revolutionary activities.

221 Dinerstein, H[erbert].S. WAR AND THE SOVIET UNION: NUCLEAR WEAPONS AND THE REVOLUTION IN SOVIET MILITARY AND POLITICAL THINKING. New York: Frederick A. Praeger, 1962. 265 p.

> The author analyzes Soviet literature on war and international conflict with focus on the relationship between communist and capitalist states. Included are descriptions of the Soviet view of the reliability of deterrence; the conduct of a nuclear war; and surprise and the initiation of war.

222 Earle, Edward Meade, ed. MAKERS OF MODERN STRATEGY: MILITARY THOUGHT FROM MACHIAVELLI TO HITLER. New York: Atheneum, 1970. 553 p.

> An anthology containing twenty-one selections drawn from writings, old and modern, on the origins of war and military strategy. Among the subjects examined in this volume are the

Military Strategy and Deterrence

impact of science and technology on war; the economic foundations of national power; the strategic thought of Karl von Clausewitz; doctrines of sea power; theories of air warfare; and Soviet and Nazi concepts of war.

223 Gallois, Pierre. THE BALANCE OF TERROR: STRATEGY FOR THE NUCLEAR AGE. Boston: Houghton Mifflin Co., 1961. 234 p.

A seminal analysis of nuclear strategy, deterrence, and alliances and the role of smaller nuclear forces. The author contends that the effect of the possession of nuclear weapons by both the United States and the Soviet Union is to render alliances obsolete, since no nation-state will use its atomic capabilities, unless its own national survival is at stake. Developing a concept of proportional deterrence, Gallois sets forth a rationale for the acquisition of nuclear weapons by smaller powers, such as France.

224 Gareau, Frederick H., ed. THE BALANCE OF POWER AND NUCLEAR DETERRENCE: A BOOK OF READINGS. Boston: Houghton Mifflin Co., 1962. 216 p.

An anthology containing twenty-two older and recent writings on the balance of power and its application in a historic European context and in the post-World War II period. A major portion of the volume is devoted to an analysis of the role of nuclear power in deterring conflict and a comparison of power balances in the atomic and pre-atomic ages.

225 George, Alexander L., and Smoke, Richard. DETERRENCE IN AMERICAN FOREIGN POLICY: THEORY AND PRACTICE. New York: Columbia University Press, 1974. 666 p.

An analysis and critique of deterrence, both in theory and practice, in American foreign policy since World War II. The authors describe in detail the nature of contemporary deterrence theory and illustrate its operation in case studies, including the Berlin blockade of 1948-49; the outbreak of the Korean War; the Taiwan Strait crisis; the Hungarian Revolution; the Middle East in 1957 and 1958; and the Cuban Missile Crisis of 1962. A major portion of the volume is devoted to a reformulation of deterrence theory.

226 Gray, Richard B., ed. INTERNATIONAL SECURITY SYSTEMS: CONCEPTS AND MODELS OF WORLD ORDER. Itasca, Ill.: F.E. Peacock Publishers, 1969. 227 p.

Twelve essays on the nature of international security systems, some of which are published for the first time in this volume. Included are such topics as bipolarity and the balance of power; alliance systems; the United Nations, collective security, and regional security systems; international law; and the role of diplomacy in security systems.

227 Green, Philip. DEADLY LOGIC: THE THEORY OF NUCLEAR DETERRENCE. New York: Schocken Books, 1966. 361 p.

A critical examination of the assumptions and the contributions of major strategic theorists and disciplines to contemporary deterrence theory. The author assesses the nature of systems analysis and national policy; the use of game theory; rationality and decision making in deterrence relationships; and problems of ethical choice in the nuclear age.

228 Halperin, Morton H. CONTEMPORARY MILITARY STRATEGY. Boston: Little, Brown and Co., 1967. 156 p.

A concise history of the evolution of American, Soviet, and Chinese military strategy and analysis of the role of force in the nuclear age. Included are assessments of the strategy of controlled response; the nature of limited war; deterrence and defense in Europe and Asia; the challenge of revolutionary war; and approaches to arms control.

229 _____. DEFENSE STRATEGIES FOR THE SEVENTIES. Boston: Little, Brown and Co., 1971. 149 p.

A short survey of military strategies with emphasis on nuclear weapons and the deterrence of conflict. Included are analyses of the evolution of American military strategy; Soviet and Chinese military concepts; the idea of limited war; deterrence and European security; problems of deterrence and defense in Asia; and strategic arms control.

230 _____. LIMITED WAR IN THE NUCLEAR AGE. New York: John Wiley and Sons, 1963. 191 p.

A study focused on the problems of using force to attain national objectives without risking nuclear war. The author examines the nature of interaction between adversaries in the nuclear age; the relationship between nuclear forces and local war; problems of arms control; and the Korean Conflict as a case study in limited war.

231 Harkabi, Y. NUCLEAR WAR AND NUCLEAR PEACE. Jerusalem: Israel Program for Scientific Translations, 1966. 303 p.

An examination of deterrence theory drawing heavily upon American literature but presenting an analysis from an Israeli perspective. Included are the author's conception and categorization of the nature of deterrence and strategic doctrines;

limited conventional and nuclear war; nuclear weapons and NATO; nuclear proliferation and the outbreak of war; disarmament and arms control.

232 Hitch, Charles J. DECISION-MAKING FOR DEFENSE. Berkeley: University of California Press, 1965. 83 p.

A short examination of the organizational evolution of the Department of Defense; the development of concepts and methodologies for planning, programming, and budgeting; the nature of cost-effectiveness techniques; and prospects for the utilization of such approaches to achieve greater efficiencies in the allocation of resources for defense.

233 Hitch, Charles J., and McKean, Roland N. THE ECONOMICS OF DEFENSE IN THE NUCLEAR AGE. Cambridge, Mass.: Harvard University Press, 1963. 422 p.

In a seminal examination of problems of achieving efficiency in the allocation of defense resources, the authors develop a methodology for achieving "cost effectiveness" in military spending. The volume contains an analysis of such issues as the indirect effects of defense spending; institutional arrangements to promote efficiency; military research and development; and criteria for choosing policies for deterrence.

234 Ho Chi Minh. ON REVOLUTION, SELECTED GREETINGS, 1920-1966. New York: Frederick A. Praeger, 1967. 389 p.

A collection of speeches, letters, and other statements and writings on the theory and practice of revolutionary warfare focusing on Indochina under French rule and after. Included are selections dealing with the author's early, formative years in France after World War I; the founding of the Communist Party of Indochina; the Japanese occupation during World War II; the struggle against France; and the Vietnam War in the early 1960s.

235 Huntington, Samuel P., ed. CHANGING PATTERNS OF MILITARY POLITICS. New York: Free Press of Glencoe, 1962. 272 p.

A collection of theoretical essays and empirical studies devoted to an analysis of the function, and varieties, of violence in the contemporary world. The volume contains original essays on such topics as patterns of violence in world politics; the "Garrison State" hypothesis; civil and military power in the French Fourth Republic; and the politics of the National Guard.

236 Kahn, Herman. ON ESCALATION: SCENARIOS AND METAPHORS. New York: Frederick A. Praeger, 1965. 308 p.

In an important study of the dynamics of escalation in an international crisis between nuclear powers, the author utilizes the metaphor of a ladder on which his forty-four steps of escalation represent the rungs. Kahn makes use of historical examples as well as hypothetical conflict situations, to illustrate his concepts. In addition, the volume contains an analysis of the process of de-escalation and crisis termination.

237 _____. ON THERMONUCLEAR WAR. Princeton: Princeton University Press, 1961. 668 p.

A major and seminal theoretical analysis of the nature of thermonuclear war and alternative strategies available to the United States to deter or to fight a nuclear conflict, and to reduce the possibility of war by accident or as a result of miscalculation.

238 _____. THINKING ABOUT THE UNTHINKABLE. New York: Horizon Press, 1962. 254 p.

A theoretical analysis of the possible causes of nuclear war, as well as its conduct and outcome. The author examines deterrence strategies, accidental war, arms control, civil defense, and problems of postnuclear attack recovery. The volume contains a discussion of international bargaining which utilizes game theory models.

239 Kaplan, Morton A., ed. SALT: PROBLEMS AND PROSPECTS. Morristown, N.J.: General Learning Press, 1973. 251 p.

A series of nine essays completed before the signing of the 1972 accords on the limitation of strategic armaments. The contributors address themselves to such topics as comparative U.S. and Soviet deployments and doctrines; the language of arms control; the implications of SALT for NATO and European security; SALT and smaller nuclear powers; and arms control and technological change.

240 Kemp, Geoffrey, et al., eds. THE SUPERPOWERS IN A MULTINUCLEAR WORLD. Lexington: D.C. Heath and Co., 1974. 300 p.

A series of original writings on the nuclear forces of smaller powers as well as potential "Nth" countries. In addition to analyses of the Soviet-American strategic relationship, the volume contains chapters on nuclear weapons and Chinese policy; Japan's nuclear options; India's nuclear program; and strategic considerations affecting medium power nuclear forces and their targeting options.

241 Kintner, William R. PEACE AND THE STRATEGY CONFLICT. New York: Frederick A. Praeger, 1967. 264 p.

>   An examination of the evolution of American and Soviet strategic forces from the end of World War II to the mid-1960s. Included are analyses of differences between superpower conceptions of strategy and nuclear weapons; the relationship between technology and power; problems of arms control; the impact of strategic parity on NATO; and the prerequisites for American strategic adequacy.

242 Kintner, William R., and Pfaltzgraff, Robert L., Jr., eds. SALT: IMPLICATIONS FOR ARMS CONTROL IN THE 1970'S. Pittsburgh: University of Pittsburgh Press, 1973. 447 p.

>   A presentation of the problems of arms control with emphasis on the negotiations leading to the SALT I accords of 1972. Among the topics considered in essays in this volume are the rationale for superpower arms control; Soviet and American interests in SALT; technological change and the strategic arms race; bargaining aspects of arms control; the American-Soviet-Chinese triangle; SALT and smaller nuclear powers and potential "Nth" countries; and the implications of SALT for international security.

243 Kintner, William R., and Scott, Harriet Fast, eds. THE NUCLEAR REVOLUTION IN SOVIET MILITARY AFFAIRS. Norman: University of Oklahoma Press, 1968. 420 p.

>   An anthology containing translations of twenty-seven of the most authoritative Soviet military writings. Included are selections on such topics as the doctrinal legacy of Khrushchev; new weapons and the duration of war; the adaptation of the writings of Clausewitz to nuclear conflict; Soviet views on military-technological superiority; the nature of modern combat; and the role and future of land forces.

244 Kissinger, Henry A. NUCLEAR WEAPONS AND FOREIGN POLICY. New York: Harper and Brothers for the Council on Foreign Relations, 1957. 463 p.

>   A review of the evolution of American strategic thought in the decade following World War II, focusing on the dilemma facing the United States in the late 1950s in designing its defense forces in light of the development by the Soviet Union of intercontinental ballistic missiles. Concerned with the creation of a strategy in support of American diplomacy without necessarily risking resort to strategic nuclear weapons, the author develops a concept for limited war and the deterrence of conflict by means of a defense posture that incorporates tactical nuclear weapons. Included is an assessment of the implications

of the proposed limited war concept for American relations with adversaries, allies, and the uncommitted nations.

245 _____, ed. PROBLEMS OF NATIONAL STRATEGY: A BOOK OF READINGS. New York: Frederick A. Praeger, 1965. 477 p.

An anthology of readings on American defense policy, with selections on strategic doctrine; quantitative analysis and national security; escalation; the problem of insurgency; alliances in the nuclear age; arms control and disarmament; antiballistic missile defense; nuclear-sharing and NATO; and governmental organization for the conduct of national security. Among the contributors are Herman Kahn, Albert Wohlstetter, Robert L. McNamara, Alan Enthoven, Thomas C. Schelling, Samuel P. Huntington, Robert R. Bowie, J.K. Zawodny, Bernard Brodie, Alastair Buchan, and Pierre Gallois.

246 Knorr, Klaus. MILITARY POWER AND POTENTIAL. Lexington, Mass.: D.C. Heath and Co., 1970. 150 p.

A good analysis of military power, in its actual and punitive dimensions, especially conditions for effective utilization of military power in relations among nations. The author categorizes the major components of administrative capacity and the political foundations of military power, and assesses the problems of measuring military power.

247 Legault, Albert, and Lindsey, George. THE DYNAMICS OF THE NUCLEAR BALANCE. Ithaca, N.Y. Cornell University Press, 1974. 273 p.

The authors describe the nature of nuclear energy and strategic weapons systems and present an analysis of theories of deterrence and arms control. Included are chapters on such topics as nuclear explosives, offensive strategic missiles and ballistic missile defense, strategic bombers and air defense, and the strategic arms limitation talks.

248 Levine, Robert A. THE ARMS DEBATE. Cambridge, Mass.: Harvard University Press, 1963. 347 p.

The author surveys and divides into five major schools the spectrum of thought of the early 1960s on American defense policy. The author describes the assumptions and value judgments, the analyses of war, power, allies, opponents, and neutrals, and the policy recommendations contained in the writings of proponents of each of the five schools of thought.

249 MccGwire, Michael, et al,, eds. SOVIET NAVAL POLICY: OBJECTIVES AND CONSTRAINTS. New York: Frederick A. Praeger, 1975. 663 p.

A collection of original essays dealing with Soviet naval strategy and forces. Special emphasis is placed on criteria for measuring "influence" and assessing economic "burden" as well as analytic tools for studying decision-making processes in Soviet defense policy.

250 Mao Tse-tung. ON GUERRILLA WARFARE. Translated by Samuel B. Griffith. New York: Frederick A. Praeger, 1961. 114 p.

The preeminent twentieth-century theorist and practitioner of guerrilla warfare sets forth his conception of strategy and tactics in a translation of a work first published in 1937. Mao defines guerrilla warfare, discusses the relationship between guerrilla hostilities and regular operations, examines the political problems of guerrilla warfare, and considers the prerequisites for victory by guerrilla operations. The volume contains an extensive introduction by the translator.

251 Morgenstern, Oskar. THE QUESTION OF NATIONAL DEFENSE. New York: Random House, 1959. 306 p.

A theoretical analysis of the nature of, and requirements for, deterrence in the nuclear age. The author examines the concept of strategic parity; defense and retaliation; methods for decreasing the vulnerability of retaliatory forces; the limitation of war; technological innovation and strategic power; and the role of diplomacy in reducing the prospects for nuclear conflict.

252 Naroll, Raoul, et al. MILITARY DETERRENCE IN HISTORY: A PILOT CROSS-HISTORICAL SURVEY. Albany: State University of New York Press, 1974. 416 p.

A survey of the theory and practice of military deterrence from ancient times to modern times. Utilizing a conceptual framework for comparative historical research, the authors develop a series of findings based on patterns common to different times and places.

253 Nef, John V. WAR AND HUMAN PROGRESS: AN ESSAY ON THE RISE OF INDUSTRIAL CIVILIZATION. Cambridge, Mass.: Harvard University Press, 1950. 464 p.

An analysis of the impact of technological innovation on the conduct of warfare from the fifteenth century to the mid-twentieth century. Special emphasis is placed on the rise of industrial civilization in Europe and the implications of new technologies for the organization of military forces, for the cost of modern warfare, and for military strategy and tactics in an age of total war.

254 Osgood, Robert E., and Tucker, Robert W. FORCE, ORDER AND JUSTICE. Baltimore: Johns Hopkins Press, 1967. 374 p.

> An examination of the role of force in international relations in historical as well as in contemporary contexts, before and after the advent of nuclear weapons. The authors analyze various rationales for the use of force and discuss the moral dilemmas raised by the existence of nuclear weapons in contrast to the military capabilities of previous eras.

255 Pfaltzgraff, Robert L., Jr., ed. CONTRASTING APPROACHES TO STRATEGIC ARMS CONTROL. Lexington, Mass.: D.C. Heath and Co., 1974. 350 p.

> An analysis of major issues of strategic arms control with special emphasis on the phase following the SALT accords of May 1972 and preceding the guidelines worked out by the United States and the Soviet Union in November 1974. Included are fourteen original essays on such topics as political and negotiating asymmetries; bureaucracies and arms control; the impact of SALT I on the U.S.-Soviet strategic balance; Soviet and American interests in strategic arms limitation; the impact of SALT on European nuclear forces, the Atlantic Alliance, and the Japanese-American relationship; China and SALT II; and potential "Nth" countries.

256 Quester, George. THE POLITICS OF NUCLEAR PROLIFERATION. Baltimore: Johns Hopkins University Press, 1973. 249 p.

> An examination of the Nuclear Proliferation Treaty of 1968 and the operation of its inspection safeguards from the perspective of the superpowers, the smaller nuclear powers, and "Nth" states. Included are chapters on such countries as the United States, the Soviet Union, India, Israel, Japan, Sweden, Britain, the Federal Republic of Germany, China, and major Latin American powers.

257 Rapoport, Anatol. STRATEGY AND CONSCIENCE. New York: Schocken Books, 1969. 323 p.

> After an extensive critique of deterrence concepts, the author examines theories of rational decision making and develops a game model based on what he calls the "prisoner's dilemma." The volume represents an effort based on game theory to set forth rational models for superpower strategic relationships and arms limitation.

258 Rosecrance, Richard [N.], ed. THE FUTURE OF THE INTERNATIONAL STRATEGIC SYSTEM. San Francisco: Chandler Publishing Co., 1972. 219 p.

> A collection of essays focusing on the nature and problems of

deterrence in a multipolar world. Contributors address themselves to the concept of multipolar nuclear strategy; superpower strategic postures; and multilateral incentives for limiting international violence. Among the eleven contributors are Donald G. Brennan, Malcolm W. Hoag, Morton A. Kaplan, George H. Quester, Kenneth E. Boulding, Richard N. Gardner, and the editor.

259 Schelling, Thomas C. ARMS AND INFLUENCE. New Haven: Yale University Press, 1966. 293 p.

An analysis of the diplomacy of violence, or how countries use their capacities for violence in bargaining for advantage. The author assesses the relationship between diplomacy and various forms of force; the nature of credibility and rationality; the manipulation of risk; and the various means of signaling about capabilities and intentions between adversaries in periods of competitive armament or arms reduction.

260 _____. THE STRATEGY OF CONFLICT. New York: Oxford University Press, 1963. 309 p.

A series of essays identifying similarities between various situations of conflict and of common interest ranging from limited war between nations to interpersonal relationships. Building on game theory, the author examines the tactics utilized in bargaining communications and negotiations, and discusses the nature of strategic moves in zero-sum (competitive) and non-zero-sum (non-competitive) contexts. The volume provides a theoretical framework for an understanding of strategy at many levels of analysis.

261 Singer, J. David. DETERRENCE, ARMS CONTROL, AND DISARMAMENT: TOWARD A SYNTHESIS IN NATIONAL SECURITY POLICY. Columbus: Ohio State University Press, 1962. 279 p.

An effort to collect and organize concepts related to deterrence and to arms control and disarmament. The author defines and analyzes deterrence and its capability requirements, relating them to arms control and disarmament as a means, respectively, of stabilizing and modifying a deterrence environment.

262 Snyder, Glenn H. DETERRENCE AND DEFENSE: TOWARD A THEORY OF NATIONAL SECURITY. Princeton: Princeton University Press, 1961. 294 p.

A contribution to the literature of the early 1960s on the development of a theory of deterrence and criteria for rational defense decision making. The author examines such topics as the logic of deterrence, the nature of uncertainty in deterring conflict; counter-force and counter-city retaliation; deterrence and alliance relationships; the defense of regions outside Europe; and the reconciliation of strategies of defense and deterrence.

263 Sokolovskiy, V.D. SOVIET MILITARY STRATEGY. Translated and edited by Harriet Fast Scott. 3d ed. New York: Crane, Russak & Co. for the Strategic Studies Center, Stanford Research Institute, 1975. 494 p.

> First published in 1968 under the title VOYENNAYA STRATE-GIYA, this volume is a translation of a comprehensive statement of Soviet military strategy with extensive annotations and analyses by American students of Soviet affairs. This edition contains chapters on the evolution of general Soviet concepts; the relationship between strategy and politics, and between strategy and economics; the nature of modern war; methods of conducting nuclear conflict; and an examination of the command structure of Soviet military forces.

264 Sprout, Harold, and Sprout, Margaret. THE RISE OF AMERICAN NAVAL POWER, 1776-1918. Princeton, N.J.: Princeton University Press, 1939. 398 p.

> An examination of the evolution of American naval policy and the emergence of the United States as a leading sea power. Included is an analysis of the writings and theories of Alfred Thayer Mahan and their implications for American naval capabilities and strategy in the twentieth century.

265 _____. TOWARD A NEW ORDER OF SEA POWER: AMERICAN NAVAL POLICY AND THE WORLD SCENE, 1918-1922. New York: Greenwood Press, 1969. 336 p.

> The authors trace the evolution of American naval policy in the early twentieth century with emphasis on the period between the end of World War I and events leading to the Washington Conference of 1922. Together with an examination of American attitudes and policies toward naval power, the volume contains extensive treatment of the Washington Conference, which was of landmark significance in establishing limitations on naval armaments in the interwar period.

266 Stanger, Roland J., ed. ESSAYS ON INTERVENTION. Columbus: Ohio State University Press, 1964. 125 p.

> An anthology containing four essays on intervention with emphasis on problems of policy and of law in the contemporary era when the distinction between violence within nations and conflict at the international level has become blurred. The volume contains analyses of the legitimacy of legislative intervention by the United Nations, the legal regulation of international coercion, and the justification for intervention. The contributors include Roger Fisher, Richard A. Falk, Michael A. Cardozo, and William T. Burke.

267 Strausz-Hupé, Robert, et al. PROTRACTED CONFLICT. New York: Harper and Row, 1963. 229 p.

> An examination of communism as a doctrine and technique of conflict, rather than as a social or economic ideology. The authors assess "protracted conflict" as a historical phenomenon in a revolutionary setting and trace the evolution of communist strategy focusing principally on the Soviet Union. Much of the volume is devoted to an analysis of communist conflict techniques and principles for the conduct of conflict adduced from the foreign policy behavior of the Soviet Union.

268 Vincent, R.J. NONINTERVENTION AND INTERNATIONAL ORDER. Princeton, N.J.: Princeton University Press, 1974. 457 p.

> A study that traces the history of the principle of nonintervention from ancient times to the present, with special emphasis on its operation and limitations in the twentieth century, and its place in international law and in the practice of statecraft. Among the topics treated are Soviet and American doctrines and practices, and the implications of technological change, ideological conflict, and the permeability of national frontiers for the principle of nonintervention.

269 Von Clausewitz, Carl. ON WAR. 3 vols. London: Kegan Paul, Trench, Truehmer and Co., 1911. 1,077 p.

> A seminal analysis of the relationship between war and politics and the theory and practice of armed conflict by an early nineteenth-century Prussian strategist whose work greatly influenced Lenin. Among the topics considered are the nature of offense and defense; the elements of strategy; the character of modern battle; retreat after the loss of a battle; the strategic means of utilizing victory; and ends-means relationships in politics and war.

270 Wilkinson, Paul. POLITICAL TERRORISM. New York: John Wiley and Sons, 1974. 160 p.

> An examination of the concepts of terror and terrorism in both historical and contemporary contexts. The author surveys terrorist movements from the eleventh century to the present and evaluates major theories and models concerning the causes, the recruitment of supporters, and the essential conditions for the success and reasons for the failure of terrorism.

271 Willrich, Mason, and Rhinelander, John B., eds. SALT: THE MOSCOW AGREEMENTS AND BEYOND. New York: Free Press, 1974. 361 p.

> A collection of ten original writings focused on the 1972 agreements for the limitation of strategic armaments. Included

are essays on the Helsinki and Vienna talks leading to the 1972 accords; a comparison of U.S. and Soviet strategic forces; Soviet and U.S. perspectives and decision making on arms control; problems of verification; European, Chinese, and Japanese views on SALT; and an appraisal of the agreements and the prospects for future accords.

272 Young, Oran R. THE POLITICS OF FORCE: BARGAINING DURING INTERNATIONAL CRISES. Princeton, N.J.: Princeton University Press, 1968. 438 p.

The author develops a conceptual framework in order to study how nations utilize political influence to achieve objectives during international crises; he tests his propositions by analyzing the following: the Berlin crises of 1948-49 and 1961; the Taiwan Strait crisis of 1958; and the Cuban Missile Crisis of 1962. He also examines the bases of international bargaining; problems of communication; restraints on the use of violence; and the role of central and peripheral actors.

Chapter 7
THEORIES OF CONFLICT

The emergence of international relations as a field of study resulted from a perceived need to develop greater understanding of the causes of conflict. Yet there has not emerged a single general theory to explain all of the varieties of conflict; and the prospects for such theoretical and methodological breakthroughs are not great. A general theory of conflict would necessarily include contributions from numerous and diverse disciplines, such as political science, history, anthropology, economics, and psychology and would encompass each of the levels of analysis of international relations study.

In the aftermath of World War I, theorists saw the roots of conflict in the pursuit of power politics by nations. According to utopian theory, however, man, by his nature, was inherently good and if his energies could be directed according to a higher morality established under international law and organization, nations would replace competition and conflict with cooperation and peace. The establishment of the League of Nations, with its collective security system, was considered to be integral to the maintenance of world peace since it would presumably provide a framework, or a higher standard, for the conduct of international relations.

In the interwar period, and even before World War I, efforts were made to establish a relationship between economics and conflict, and to study the nature of imperialism and its implications for international conflict. In addition, pioneering work on the relationship between conflict and the individual was begun.[1] Scholars began to develop theories of conflict based upon the psychology of the individual. For example, the frustration-aggression hypothesis of psychologists such as Dollard and Doob suggested that aggressive behavior could be traced to frustration in the pursuit of an objective.[2]

---

[1] See, for example, Harold D. Lasswell, WORLD POLITICS AND PERSONAL INSECURITY (No. 301).

[2] See, for example, John Dollard, Leonard W. Doob, Neal E. Miller, et al., FRUSTRATION AND AGGRESSION (New Haven: Yale University Press, 1939).

Theories of Conflict

While it is plausible to hypothesize a relationship between conflicts inside the psychic structure of the individual and conflict in the international system, there is not sufficient evidence to suggest that international conflict can be explained only, or even largely, in terms of inner psychic forces. Other scholars have sought explanations of international conflict at the level of the nation-state.[3] There have been studies, for example, focusing upon the clash of national interests, the growth of expansionist nationalisms and ideologies, and the relationship between domestic political structure and conflict among nations. Students of nationalism have noted the extent to which modern nationalism provided greater cohesiveness within national boundaries and led, as in the case of Austria-Hungary and the Ottoman Empire, to the breakdown of multinational empires.[4] Still other scholars have sought an explanation of conflict in the development of action-reaction models for the analysis of arms races and of decision-making behavior during crisis situations.[5] Arms decisions on one side allegedly produce countervailing decisions by the other side. However, scholars are in disagreement as to the validity of action-reaction models in the study of conflict. If World War I was alleged to have resulted from an arms race between opposing alliance systems, World War II has often been explained as the result of the lack of adequate levels of armaments among those who opposed Hitler's expansionism.

Studies of conflict have focused on such phenomena as political alienation and relative deprivation, especially in the analysis of revolution.[6] It has been suggested that revolutionary behavior results from the alienation of individuals and groups from the political system. Other scholars have hypothesized, in studies based upon a concept of relative deprivation, that improvements within a society that are not widely shared, or that do not continue at an even pace, can produce disturbance leading perhaps to revolution. Studies of revolutionary behavior have formed an important part of the literature of international conflict. Such studies include the analysis of so-called "linkages" between the international environment and the societies in which revolutionary behavior occurs.[7] For example, scholars have concerned themselves with the impact of intervention by outside powers upon revolutionary movements within societies. The extent to which revolutionary activity in one country contributes to revolution in other countries--its so-called "demonstration effect"--has interested scholars in their studies of conflict behavior.

---

[3] See, for example, No. 325 for an analysis of theories of the nation-state, the international system, and the individual and conflict.

[4] See Nos. 96 and 97.

[5] See Nos. 312 and 313.

[6] See Nos. 286 and 293.

[7] See, for example, Nos. 309, 315, 323, 326, and 327.

Theories of Conflict

The study of conflict, as noted earlier, has drawn heavily upon conceptualization from a variety of disciplines outside political science. Methodologically, the study of conflict has been greatly influenced by quantitative analysis over the past generation. Building upon the pioneering work of Lewis F. Richardson on arms races,[8] more recent scholars have examined the relationship between the formation of alliances and the outbreak of war, the role of peacekeeping organizations in the resolution of conflict, the relationship between patterns of economic development and conflict behavior and the precise patterns of interaction among decision makers within and between opposing alliances during crisis periods leading to the outbreak of war.[9]

Quantitatively oriented scholars, like many other students of conflict, have concerned themselves in some instances with the interplay of domestic and international factors in the study of conflict. There have been studies of the hypothesized effects of the level of economic development, the size of a country, the density of population, and the level of national violence, to mention but a few of the categories in which data about internal behavior have been collected. Efforts have been made to assess the implications of domestic behavior for foreign policy and especially for the propensity of nation-states to engage in international conflict.

Scholars have long been concerned about the relationship between the structure of the international system and conflict among nations. Those who criticized balance of power often saw in this international system structure an inherent tendency toward conflict. In contrast proponents of one or another variant of balance of power have usually held that a distribution of capabilities among several nations reduces the likelihood of conflict among them or at least holds it within manageable bounds. Much of the literature of international relations on alternative conceptions of world order has as its focal point the implications of such structure for the reduction of conflict among nations or other constituent groups into which the world is, or would be, divided. Thus, the analysis of the international system, both as it exists or as it might evolve in the future, places emphasis on conflict behavior.

There is little agreement among scholars as to the causes of conflict among nations or the prerequisites for its resolution. It is uncertain as to whether a single model or theory of conflict would be adequate to explain the varieties of conflict among human beings in general and even at the international level. Nor is there agreement as to whether conflict is completely disintegrative or if it provides an integrative force. Some scholars, for example, have viewed conflict as a means of increasing the cohesiveness of one group against another, as contrasted with integration theory--to be discussed in another section--in which

---

[8]Lewis F. Richardson, ARMS AND INSECURITY (No. 312).

[9]See, for example, Nos. 281, 317, and 321.

Theories of Conflict

the integration of political communities is alleged to provide an alternative to conflict.[10]

Whatever the answers to such questions, the need to study more systematically the causes of conflict will remain urgent. The continued development of unprecedented means of destruction, the persistence of old conflict issues within and among nations, and the emergence of new conflict-laden problems will challenge both the scholar and the policymaker to develop a more adequate understanding of the nature of conflict in the years ahead.

273 Ardrey, Robert. THE TERRITORIAL IMPERATIVE: A PERSONAL INQUIRY INTO THE ANIMAL ORIGINS OF PROPERTY AND NATIONS. New York: Atheneum, 1966. 390 p.

> An important examination of the evolutionary nature of man in which the author compares patterns of aggression and conflict in human beings and in animals. The findings are based on scientific observations of territorial behavior in animals as well as on insights drawn from biology.

274 Arendt, Hannah. ON VIOLENCE. New York: Harcourt, Brace and World, 1970. 106 p.

> An analysis of major theories of violence in historical perspective and an assessment of the nature and manifestations of violence in the present world, together with the author's examination of the relationship between war and politics, violence and power.

275 Beitz, Charles R., and Herman, Theodore, eds. PEACE AND WAR. San Francisco: W.H. Freeman and Co., 1973. 435 p.

> An anthology designed primarily for undergraduate use containing twenty-nine selections on the nature of war and the building of a more peaceful world, many drawn from the literature of "peace research." Among the topics examined are the moral logic of war; the diplomacy of violence; causes of conflict; models of world order; the nature of nonviolence; and strategic choices.

276 Ben-Dak, Joseph D., ed. THE FUTURE OF COLLECTIVE VIOLENCE: SOCIETAL AND INTERNATIONAL PERSPECTIVES. New York: Humanities Press, 1974. 215 p.

> A collection of ten writings containing theoretical and empirical research on violence. Among the topics examined are the

---

[10]See, for example, Nos. 283 and 284.

role of anxiety and cleavage in violence: attitudes toward, and justifications for, violence; the idea of nonviolent action as a substitute for violence; and linkages between domestic and international violence.

277　Blainey, Geoffrey. THE CAUSES OF WAR. New York: Free Press, 1975. 278 p.

A survey of all international wars fought since 1700. The author examines the factors that have led nations to enter conflicts and presents a critique of existing theories of war. Included is an analysis of varieties of war, as well as an assessment of the impact of technology on the propensity for, and the intensity and duration of, international conflict.

278　Bloomfield, Lincoln, and Leiss, Amelia C. CONTROLLING SMALL WARS: A STRATEGY FOR THE 1970'S. New York: Alfred A. Knopf, 1969. 421 p.

The authors compare and contrast limited conflicts since World War II, draw conclusions concerning the structure of small wars, and set forth implications for American strategy. Included are analyses of the Soviet-Iranian conflict, the Bay of Pigs, the Greek insurgency, the Indonesian War of Independence, and the Middle East conflict.

279　Boulding, Kenneth E., and Mukerjee, Tapan, eds. ECONOMIC IMPERIALISM: A BOOK OF READINGS. Ann Arbor: University of Michigan Press, 1972. 338 p.

An anthology containing fifteen older and contemporary writings and an extensive bibliography on imperialism. Included are selections on such topics as the dynamics and nature of imperialism; the impact of British rule on the Indian economy; Russian imperialism; and the burdens and benefits of empire.

280　Cantril, Hadley, ed. TENSIONS THAT CAUSE WARS. Urbana: University of Illinois Press, 1951. 303 p.

A collection of writings dealing with social-psychological factors that are held to affect international conflict. Contributors seek to relate tensions among nations to individual behavior and to develop propositions and analogies about international relations based on stereotypes, perceptions, and the psychological characteristics of individuals.

281　Choucri, Nazli, and North, Robert C. NATIONS IN CONFLICT: NATIONAL GROWTH AND INTERNATIONAL VIOLENCE. San Francisco: W.H. Freeman and Co., 1975. 356 p.

An effort to study the causes of World War I by the analysis of data about the fluctuation in violence among great powers, with special emphasis on changes in population, technology, trade, military expenditures, colonial territory, and alliances. The authors develop a conceptual framework which provides for the use of computer simulations, as well as the writings of historians, the memoirs of national leaders, and archives, in order to study the historical process leading to the outbreak of the First World War.

282 Cohen, Benjamin J. THE QUESTION OF IMPERIALISM: THE POLITICAL ECONOMY OF DOMINANCE AND DEPENDENCE. New York: Basic Books, 1973. 280 p.

A good critique of theories of imperialism from Lenin to the radical left of the 1960s. The author examines the meaning of imperialism, including the idea of dependence and exploitation, and sets forth his own framework for a general theory of imperialism.

283 Coser, Lewis A. CONTINUITIES IN THE STUDY OF SOCIAL CONFLICT. New York: Free Press, 1967. 272 p.

Building upon his earlier writings, the author examines the role of conflict in the integration of societies, assesses types of conflict marked by violence, and applies conflict theory to the study of contemporary political problems. The volume contains extended treatment of the prospects for new nations; disintegration within the communist world; and a critique of the conflict theories of Karl Marx and Emile Durkheim.

284 _____. THE FUNCTIONS OF SOCIAL CONFLICT. New York: Free Press, 1956. 188 p.

An important study designed to clarify and synthesize conceptual designs and to present the author's own framework for the study of social conflict. Special emphasis is placed on the role of conflict in contributing to group cohesiveness; on the nature of conflict within groups; and on conflict with other groups.

285 Crosier, Brian. A THEORY OF CONFLICT. New York: Charles Scribner's Sons, 1974. 245 p.

A good analysis of conflict both in its historical and contemporary manifestations. The author assesses causes and techniques of revolution, with emphasis on nuclear terrorism and hijacking, as well as the countermeasures that can be adopted by states. Examples are drawn from revolutionary movements to illustrate the thesis developed in the study.

Theories of Conflict

286 Davies, James Chowning, ed. WHEN MEN REVOLT--AND WHY: A READER IN POLITICAL VIOLENCE AND REVOLUTION. New York: Free Press, 1971. 357 p.

>A collection of writings presenting a broad range of theories and strategies designed to explain the nature of revolution and how individuals and societies meet the challenge of change. Selections from works on general theory, ancient and contemporary, are included. Several contributors consider the role of psychological factors in revolutionary behavior. A major portion of the volume is devoted to readings containing the results of recent social science research.

287 Dunn, Frederick Sherwood. PEACEFUL CHANGE: A STUDY OF INTERNATIONAL PROCEDURES. New York: Council on Foreign Relations, 1937. 156 p.

>An examination of major categories of issues such as economic disparities, raw materials deficiencies, population pressure, and ethnic problems, which give rise to disputes and conflicts among nations. The author discusses procedures for peaceful change, including diplomatic negotiation, conciliation, international conferences, adjudication, and commissions of inquiry.

288 Eckstein, Harry, ed. INTERNAL WAR: PROBLEMS AND APPROACHES. New York: Free Press of Glencoe, 1964. 339 p.

>A collection of twelve writings on the origins, nature, types, and objectives of internal wars. Among the topics considered are the place of force in the social process; terror as a weapon of political agitation; external involvement in internal war; rebellion and political development; economic aspects of revolutions; and the role of political commitment in national revolutions.

289 Finlay, David J., et al. ENEMIES IN POLITICS. Chicago: Rand McNally and Co., 1967. 257 p.

>A discussion based on a theoretical framework and research about the ways in which enemies are defined in national and international politics. The authors present an analysis based on studies of John Foster Dulles' interpretations of Soviet foreign policy; the role of enemies during Nkrumah's rule in Ghana; and Castro's conception of the enemies of his government in Cuba.

290 Fisher, Roger. INTERNATIONAL CONFLICT FOR BEGINNERS. New York: Harper and Row, 1969. 231 p.

>A short primer, or how-to-do-it guide, for the statesman and the student of international affairs. The author examines and

critiques some of the premises on which foreign policies are based, and illustrates his analysis by reference to such problem areas as Vietnam, Korea, Cuba, Rhodesia, and the Middle East.

291 _____, ed. INTERNATIONAL CONFLICT AND BEHAVIORAL SCIENCE. New York: Basic Books, 1974. 281 p.

A collection of writings by eminent authors on such topics as Soviet and American perceptions; strategic thought; the crisis of the nation-state; decision making in conflict situations; nonlethal equivalents of war; and problems of conflict management and reduction.

292 Fried, Morton, et al., eds. WAR: THE ANTHROPOLOGY OF ARMED CONFLICT AND AGGRESSION. Garden City, N.Y.: Natural History Press, 1968. 262 p.

A collection of essays devoted to an examination of such issues as the biological effects of war; the nature of human aggression; distinctions between primitive and modern war; psychological dimensions of war; and the implications of conflict for social structure.

293 Gurr, Ted Robert. WHY MEN REBEL. Princeton, N.J.: Princeton University Press, 1970. 421 p.

An important analysis of the nature and causes of political violence based on theories and research from the social sciences. The author examines hypotheses about relative deprivation and its intensity and scope, as well as rising expectations, and presents his findings about political violence.

294 Hobson, J.A. IMPERIALISM: A STUDY. 3d ed. London: George Allen & Unwin, 1948. 386 p.

A seminal but controversial analysis and critique of imperialism which greatly influenced Lenin's thought on the same subject (see entry 302). Basing his analysis principally on Britain, Hobson contends that imperialism, however profitable for certain groups, does not benefit the nation as a whole, while it exploits peoples in overseas territories.

295 Holsti, Ole R. CRISIS, ESCALATION, WAR. Montreal: McGill-Queen's University Press, 1972. 290 p.

Based on the crisis culminating in the outbreak of World War II and the Cuban Missile Crisis of 1962, the author compares and contrasts processes of escalation, perceptions by decision makers, communications patterns, and decision-making environments. Emphasis is placed on indicators of perceived levels of

Theories of Conflict

hostility and policy alternatives, communications within and between alliances, stress and time pressure, and the military capabilities and strategies of crisis adversaries. The author relies heavily on quantitative indicators to test hypotheses about crisis behavior.

296 Jervis, Robert. THE LOGIC OF IMAGES IN INTERNATIONAL RELATIONS. Princeton, N.J.: Princeton University Press, 1970. 281 p.

An analysis of the ways in which nations attempt to transmit desired images and to influence the images of themselves held by other nations. Applying his analysis to U.S.-Soviet relations and the Vietnam War, the author assesses the use of ambiguity, the substantive acts of nations, and signals of various kinds in the mutual development of images. He treats deception as an integral part of international relations and attempts to set forth concepts and propositions from which a theory of deception could be developed.

297 Johnson, Chalmers. REVOLUTIONARY CHANGE. Boston: Little Brown and Co., 1966. 191 p.

The author develops a model based on a synthesis of "coercion" and "value" theories of society for the study of revolution. Included are analyses of strategies and varieties of revolution; the structure and function of social systems; and the measurement of equilibrium and disequilibrium.

298 Kelman, Herbert C., ed. INTERNATIONAL BEHAVIOR: A SOCIAL-PSYCHOLOGICAL ANALYSIS. New York: Holt, Rinehart and Winston, 1965. 626 p.

A volume designed to bring together literature focused on the social-psychological processes related to interaction between governments with special emphasis on elites and the general public. In sixteen writings, authors explore such topics as the potential and limitations of social-psychological approaches; socialization, social structure, and intersocietal images; images in the context of international conflict; decision making; bargaining and negotiation; and definition of the situation as a determinant of international action.

299 Keynes, John Maynard. THE ECONOMIC CONSEQUENCES OF THE PEACE. New York: Harcourt, Brace and Howe, 1920. 298 p.

A critique of the Treaty of Versailles based on an analysis of its reparations clauses and the impact of World War I on the economies of Germany and other European countries. The author examines the pre-World War I European economic system and presents a first-hand account of the Paris Peace Conference.

Theories of Conflict

300   Klineberg, Otto. THE HUMAN DIMENSION IN INTERNATIONAL RELATIONS. New York: Holt, Rinehart and Winston, 1964. 173 p.

       An examination of the nature of human aggressiveness and war, the myth of race, the idea of national character, and the role of stereotypes. In an effort to contribute to an understanding of international conflict, the author draws heavily on theories, insights, and methodologies utilized in the study of psychology.

301   Lasswell, Harold D. WORLD POLITICS AND PERSONAL INSECURITY. New York: Free Press, 1965. 228 p.

       Drawing heavily on social-psychological theories, the author depicts wars and revolutions as mechanisms for the discharge of collective mass insecurities and tensions. Central to the analysis are national symbols and value systems. Included is an examination of the relationship between psychological analysis and the balance of power, international crises, imperialism, war, nationalism, and international organization.

302   Lenin, V.I. IMPERIALISM: THE HIGHEST STAGE OF CAPITALISM. New York: International Publishers, 1939. 128 p.

       A controversial, yet influential, writing setting forth Lenin's theory concerning the evolution and nature of imperialism in capitalist societies and providing an important contribution to communist theory of conflict and of international relations. The author relates imperialism to conflict among nations and draws heavily on the work of the English writer, J.A. Hobson (see entries 206 and 294).

303   _____. STATE AND REVOLUTION. New York: International Publishers, 1932. 103 p.

       One of the most important of Lenin's writings setting forth his theory of class conflict, the "withering away of the state," revolution, the nature of just and unjust wars, and the self-determination of nationalities. The volume also contains Lenin's description of the split within the international communist movement resulting from World War I, as well as attitudes of political parties in Russia on the eve of the Russian Revolution.

304   Lichtheim, George. IMPERIALISM. New York: Frederick A. Praeger, 1971. 183 p.

       The author traces the evolution of imperialism from ancient Rome to the twentieth century, including the post-World War II period. Included are his analyses of such concepts as nationalism, mercantilism, liberalism, and capitalism, as well as a critique of the writings on imperialism of Marx, Kautsky, Lenin, Hobson, Hilferding, Schumpeter, and the New Left writers of the 1960s.

Theories of Conflict

305   Lorenz, Konrad. ON AGGRESSION. New York: Harcourt, Brace and World, Inc., 1963. 306 p.

An analysis of conflict and aggression based on detailed observation and explanation of aggression in forms of life other than man. Hypothesizing that aggression is instinctive, Lorenz describes the forces giving rise to aggressive behavior in animals, and the ways in which animals limit their aggressive tendencies in the interest of species preservation. Lorenz concludes that aggressive behavior in human beings--and in animals--cannot be eliminated, but only directed toward harmless pursuits.

306   McNeil, Elton B., ed. THE NATURE OF HUMAN CONFLICT. Englewood Cliffs, N.J.: Prentice-Hall, 1965. 315 p.

An anthology of social science literature on conflict at the national and international levels. Among the fifteen selections included are writings on the nature of aggression and on human conflict from the points of view of anthropology, psychology, and history, as well as an assessment of the contributions to the study of conflict of political science, economics, game theory, systems theory, and decision-making theory.

307   May, Rollo. POWER AND INNOCENCE: A SEARCH FOR THE SOURCES OF VIOLENCE. New York: W.W. Norton and Co., 1972. 283 p.

An examination by a psychotherapist of the nature, meaning, and kinds of violence. May emphasizes the psychology of aggression and the psychoneurological aspects of violence, and urges the development of a new ethic in place of existing values.

308   Meisel, James H. COUNTERREVOLUTION: HOW REVOLUTIONS DIE. New York: Atherton Press, 1966. 237 p.

An examination of revolutionary movements and their leaders from the ancient world to the twentieth century. The author assesses revolution as a movement among intellectuals and surveys revolutionary movements in the Roman Empire, seventeenth-century England, eighteenth-century France, and twentieth-century Europe.

309   Midlarsky, Manus I. ON WAR: POLITICAL VIOLENCE IN THE INTERNATIONAL SYSTEM. New York: Free Press, 1975. 229 p.

An examination of the circumstances in which the outbreak of war is most likely, based on statistical analyses of the war experiences of more than one hundred countries between 1815 and 1945. The author utilizes three levels of analysis--within the international system, within the nation-state, and within the boundary of state, focusing on group and individual behavior--to seek tentative answers to major questions such as:

the relationship between alliances and wars; the contribution of peacekeeping organizations to the reduction of conflict; and the implications of economic development for conflict among and within nations.

310   Moon, Parker Thomas. IMPERIALISM AND WORLD POLITICS. New York: Macmillan Co., 1927. 583 p.

An early survey of the nature of imperialism in the nineteenth and early twentieth centuries within the context of a study of international politics. In addition to an analysis of the dynamics of imperialism, the author examines the policies of imperialist powers and their impacts on Africa and Asia, as well as imperialism within Europe and the Mandate system of the League of Nations.

311   Northedge, F.S., and Donelan, M.D. INTERNATIONAL DISPUTES: THE POLITICAL ASPECTS. New York: St. Martin's Press, 1971. 349 p.

The authors trace the evolution of thought on the nature of international disputes from medieval times to the twentieth century and examine the origins, development, limitation, and prevention of disputes within and between states. The volume includes an evaluation of the role of international organizations, as well as efforts at negotiation, mediation, arbitration, and adjudication.

312   Richardson, Lewis F. ARMS AND INSECURITY: A MATHEMATICAL STUDY OF THE CAUSES AND ORIGINS OF WAR. Pittsburgh: Boxwood Press, 1960. 307 p.

A pioneering effort to use mathematics in the study of international relations and an early effort to develop the so-called "action-reaction" model of arms races and wars. The author makes use of data for the periods between 1820 and 1939 concerning the economic, historical, social, and psychological factors allegedly contributing to arms races and tests hypotheses by means of differential equations.

313   _____. STATISTICS OF DEADLY QUARRELS. Pittsburgh: Boxwood Press, 1960. 373 p.

A volume containing data on deadly quarrels collected from 1820 to 1945. Included are statistics on the distribution of wars in time; economic causes; language; religion; the number of nations on each side of a war; contiguity and deadly quarrels; together with a preliminary sketch of a theory of the occurrence of fatal quarrels. Like other writings of the author, this study represents a pioneering effort to make use of mathemathics in analysis of the causes and characteristics of wars.

Theories of Conflict

314 Robbins, Lionel. THE ECONOMIC CAUSES OF WAR. New York: Howard Fertig, 1968. 124 p.

> An important analysis and critique of major theories about the causes of war first published after the outbreak of World War II. The author examines the Marxian theory of imperialism; the role of national power and economic factors; the nature of national and sectional interests as catalysts for international conflict; the causes and consequences of economic nationalism; and the meaning of economic causation in historical explanation.

315 Rosenau, James N. INTERNATIONAL ASPECTS OF CIVIL STRIFE. Princeton, N.J.: Princeton University Press, 1964. 322 p.

> A collection of nine original essays focused on the interplay between domestic and international factors affecting civil strife within nations. Among the topics examined are the role of outside powers in internal war; the nature and politics of intervention; modes of international settlement, and the international relations of internal war.

316 Russett, Bruce M., ed. ECONOMIC THEORIES OF INTERNATIONAL POLITICS. Chicago: Markham Publishing Co., 1968. 542 p.

> A collection of twenty-nine writings, written for the most part in the 1960s, dealing with economic theories considered to be relevant to the study of international politics. Among the topics considered are economic theories of alliances and coalitions; strategy and market structure; internal determinants of national behavior based on the study of business firms; and alternative frameworks for international decision making. An effort is made by the editor to suggest the utility and limitations of each of the economic approaches included in this volume for the study and understanding of international politics.

317 _____, ed. PEACE, WAR, AND NUMBERS. Beverly Hills, Calif.: Sage Publications, 1972. 352 p.

> A collection of eleven writings in which the authors develop and test hypotheses about the causes of international violence and suggest the relevance of their findings for theory and for the policy community. The volume contains chapters on such topics as arms levels and the incidence of war; internal and external influences on bargaining in arms control negotiations; and models for the analysis of conflict behavior among states.

318 Scott, John Paul. AGGRESSION. Chicago: University of Chicago Press, 1958. 149 p.

> An analysis of the nature of aggression and its control, with

Theories of Conflict

emphasis on heredity, social causes, and psychological factors. The author examines aggression as maladaptive behavior, the ecological causes of aggression, and the social control of aggression.

319 Simonds, Frank H., and Emeny, Brooks. THE GREAT POWERS IN WORLD POLITICS: INTERNATIONAL RELATIONS AND ECONOMIC NATIONALISM. New York: American Book Co., 1939. 731 p.

A major textbook of the interwar period focusing on economic factors, including disparities among nations, that, according to the authors, gave rise to international conflict. Included are analyses of the pre-World War II state system; the operation of the League of Nations; and the foreign policies of major powers in Europe and Asia, as well as the United States.

320 Singer, J. David, ed. HUMAN BEHAVIOR AND INTERNATIONAL POLITICS: CONTRIBUTIONS FROM THE SOCIAL PSYCHOLOGICAL SCIENCES. Chicago: Rand McNally and Co., 1965. 466 p.

A collection of writings from recent literature in anthropology, psychology, and sociology which have findings, insights, and propositions of potential value to the student of comparative foreign policy and international politics. Included are essays on the nature of the international system, the utility of systems theory, public opinion as a decisional input, the nature of power and influence, modes of conflict management, styles of conflict behavior, and system transformation.

321 Small, Melvin, and Singer, J. David. THE IMAGES OF WAR, 1816-1965: A STATISTICAL HANDBOOK. New York: John Wiley and Sons, 1972. 419 p.

A volume containing data on wars gathered by the authors for their correlates of war project. Among the data included are rankings of wars by severity, magnitude, and intensity; cycles in the incidence of war; the war-proneness of nations and regimes; and battle deaths for opposing sides in wars.

322 Smith, Clagett C., ed. CONFLICT RESOLUTION: CONTRIBUTIONS OF THE BEHAVIORAL SCIENCES. Notre Dame: University of Notre Dame Press, 1971. 553 p.

An extensive collection of essays based on conflict research undertaken since 1958. Based on personality, interpersonal, intergroup, and international analytical levels, the volume includes writings on alternative theoretical approaches; social conflict and social change; class conflict; the nature of revolutionary conflict; dimensions of conflict behavior within and between nations; conflict escalation; strategies of conflict, resolution and termination; and societal, attitudinal, and structural factors in international relations.

323 Spiegel, Steven L., and Waltz, Kenneth N., eds. CONFLICT IN WORLD POLITICS. Cambridge, Mass.: Winthrop Publishers, 1971. 474 p.

    A series of twenty-two original essays dealing with the causes and consequences of specific conflicts within and among nations. The contributors address several categories of conflict, including those between superpowers; the problems of divided countries; ethnic nationalism; internal conflicts; social-economic cooperation and conflict; and conflicts within governmental bureaucracies and political systems on policy formation and application.

324 Stoessinger, John G. WHY NATIONS GO TO WAR. New York: St. Martin's Press, 1974. 230 p.

    In six cases of twentieth-century international conflict, the author examines in detail the point at which political leaders crossed the threshold to war. In studying the outbreak of World War I; Hitler's attack on the Soviet Union; the Korean War; Vietnam; the Indo-Pakistan conflicts; and the Israeli-Arab wars, the author attempts to answer the questions of: at what moment a decision to go to war became irreversible; who bore the responsibility for such a decision, and why; and could war have been averted.

325 Waltz, Kenneth N. MAN, THE STATE, AND WAR: A THEORETICAL ANALYSIS. New York: Columbia University Press, 1959. 263 p.

    An important survey of literature on the causes of war. Basing his conceptualization on three levels of analysis--the international system, the state, and individual behavior--the author examines classical and modern writings in the following areas: the behavioral sciences; social-psychological explanations; the relationship between the internal structure of states and war; international conflict and international anarchy; and economic theories of war. An extensive bibliography is included.

326 Wilkenfeld, Jonathan, ed. CONFLICT BEHAVIOR AND LINKAGE POLITICS. New York: David McKay Co., 1973. 388 p.

    A collection of eleven writings addressed to the testing of propositions and theory building about linkages between conflict behavior in the domestic system and in the foreign policy of nations. The anthology includes chapters on societal development and international conflict; field theory and national-international linkages; and linkage models of domestic and international conflict behavior.

Theories of Conflict

327 Wright, Quincy. A STUDY OF WAR. 2d ed. Chicago: University of Chicago Press, 1965. 642 p.

> This important and monumental study of the origin and stages in the history of war and the functions of modern conflict, the development of modern military strategy, and the general characteristics of international law in the regulation of conflict, was first published in 1942. In a multidisciplinary analysis utilizing qualitative and quantitative approaches and data, the author presents a theory embodying four factors that allegedly determine the occurrence of war: technology, law, the organization of political society, and the basic values of nations and of mankind.

Chapter 8
INTEGRATION AND ALLIANCE THEORIES

Central to the study of international relations in its formative phase was the analysis of the conditions for the building of a more peaceful world order. Normative studies had as a focal point the development of proposals for international law and organization and world government. The emergence of international organizations--first the League of Nations and later the United Nations and the European Community--furnished an important source of data for scholarly investigation. Although the literature of international integration has often revealed the normative biases of its authors in favor of international organization, the emphasis of scholarship in the past generation has been upon the development of theory, the testing of hypotheses, and the utilization of innovative methodologies.

No theoretical approach has been more widely discussed in integration literature than functionalism as first developed in the study of international relations by David Mitrany.[1] Functionalism provided both a theory of integration and a strategy for the development of political community at the international level. The functionalist logic held that modern technology created problems that could only be solved by collaboration beyond the nation-state. The increasing complexity of international relationships, resulting from the pervasive influence of technology, made it necessary to entrust a wide variety of tasks to essentially apolitical technocrats. Functionalism described a phenomenon in which highly technical functions performed by technical specialists would eventually encroach upon, if not make obsolete, the political structure. Furthermore, it was suggested that successful collaboration among technical specialists in one sector would contribute to support for functional collaboration, or "spillover," in other sectors. In this respect those who favored international organization saw in functionalism not only a description of the evolving world situation but also a strategy for increasing the integration of the international community.

Subsequent generations of scholars have both refined and criticized the theoreti-

---

[1] David Mitrany, A WORKING PEACE SYSTEM (No. 353).

cal approach set forth in early functionalist literature.[2] Efforts have been made to test functionalist propositions by reference to existing international organizations such as the United Nations and the European Community. For example, it has been suggested that the extent to which "spillover" from one sector to another takes place depends upon the nature of the sector. There is no inevitable automaticity about spillover from one sector to another. In addition, the literature of the past generation reflects the efforts of scholars to develop other concepts of integration. One of the debates within the literature of integration concerns the extent to which it is possible, through a slow process of functional integration, to build a political community, as contrasted with the view that political communities emerge as a result of acts of political will. The limitations of the functionalist approach in the building of European Community institutions have contributed to the reassessment of functionalist and subsequent neo-functionalist theories of international integration.

Much of the literature of integration at the international level is closely linked to the study of integration at other levels; for example, within the nation. Scholars have hypothesized the existence of similarities, in theory at least, between integration at the international level and nation building in less developed areas and the growth of nations and nationalism within the North Atlantic area.[3] Scholars who have studied nation building have sometimes sought to extend their analyses to the building of international community, although it is by no means self evident that the integrative process at one level is similar to that at another level.

The study of integration has reflected the growth of interest in methodologies based upon quantification. Scholars have attempted to measure the development of integration by reference to indicators such as trade, the movement of people, the flow of mail and other communications, the counting of favorable references to symbols of an integrative unit, and the development of support for integration within various sectors of a population.[4] Such analyses have focused upon integration in the nation-state as well as the building of political communities at the international level. In order to measure support for integration scholars have made use of existing survey research as well as data based upon their own interviews of various samples within a population.[5]

---

[2]See, for example, Ernst B. Haas, BEYOND THE NATION-STATE (No. 342). See also Nos. 341, 343, 344, 347, 348, 349, 350, 355, 356, and 358.

[3]See Nos. 333, 334, and 337.

[4]See, for example, No. 334.

[5]See, for example, Ronald Inglehart, "An End to European Integration?" AMERICAN POLITICAL SCIENCE REVIEW 61 (March 1967), pp. 91-105.

Integration and Alliance Theories

One of the major problems discussed in the integration literature relates to the appropriate indicators for the measurement of integration. Disagreement among scholars about indicators reflects, in turn, differing definitions of integration. But it also is indicative of methodological controversy as to the value of strictly quantitative analysis. One example will suffice: should the study of European integration rest primarily upon the measurement of growth of trade and the flow of mail or is it more useful to measure the flow of official transactions such as exchanges of visits among heads of governments and other high level diplomatic interactions within Western Europe? Is the measurement of mass opinion more relevant than the analysis of elite opinion in understanding the status of, or the prospects for, political integration?

More recent studies of integration represent, for the most part, the interest of scholars in the development of definitions and theories of integration which bring together hypotheses and methodologies from earlier analyses into an innovative framework.[6] An adequate theory of integration, it is suggested, must provide for intergovernmental relationships as well as the development of support for integration at a broader mass level. While the ultimate decision-making authority rests with the legally constituted officials, the analysis of integration cannot be complete without the study of the growth of support among politically relevant strata outside the government.

Closely related to the study of integration has been the analysis of alliance behavior. Historically, alliances among nations mirrored the interests of nations in achieving higher degrees of collaboration with each other while maintaining as great a degree of independence as possible. Of great interest to scholars has been the study of the conditions leading to the formation of alliances and contributing to their cohesion as well as their ultimate disintegration. In the literature of international relations scholars have focused on such analyses of alliances by reference to historical cases[7] and more recently by the use of game theory.[8] Efforts have been made to devise models for the study of alliances from other disciplines such as economics and mathematics. As noted in the section on "Power and International Relations" the literature of conflict has contained studies of alliances because of the hypothesized relationship between the formation of alliances and the outbreak of conflict--although there is no conclusive evidence that alliances inevitably produce or prevent conflict.

Although the study of international relations has focused primarily on interstate relationships, there has been a growth of interest in transnational phenomena. The development of the multinational corporation as well as the expansion of contacts across national frontiers at a nongovernmental level has led scholars increasingly to an examination of this dimension of international studies. Schol-

---

[6] See, for example, Nos. 331, 348, 355, and 356.

[7] George Liska, NATIONS IN ALLIANCE (No. 352).

[8] William H. Riker, THE THEORY OF POLITICAL COALITIONS (No. 359).

arly interest has risen in the examination of the implications of such relationships for the study of integration at the international level.

The existence of a world faced with growing problems that cannot be resolved effectively or exclusively by the nation-state assures a prominent place in the international relations literature of the future for the study of integration. One of the many paradoxes of our age is the existence, on the one hand, of problems that defy strictly national solutions accompanied, on the other, by the persistence, and even the strengthening, of movements seeking to achieve their own autonomy or independence within, or apart from, the nation-state. In the past generation separatist movements, many of them ethnically based, have risen to prominence in all parts of the world. The age of nationalism has not given way inevitably to forces making for larger political units beyond the nation-state. Thus the problem facing scholars and policymakers will be to design frameworks that reconcile the need for larger political units with the quest for local control by the many and diverse groups into which the world is divided. If the literature of integration is to contribute to the development of such frameworks, it must reflect a synthesis between normative and analytic theory and between the qualitative and quantitative dimensions of the study of integration.

328 Ake, Claude. A THEORY OF POLITICAL INTEGRATION. Homewood, Ill.: Dorsey Press, 1967. 164 p.

> An analysis of the nature of political integration with special emphasis on the problems incurred in developing a political culture and building commitment to it. In addition to formulating his own model, the author surveys major theories of integration based either on coercion or consensus.

329 Cantori, Louis J., and Spiegel, Steven L., eds. THE INTERNATIONAL POLITICS OF REGIONS: A COMPARATIVE APPROACH. Englewood Cliffs, N.J.: Prentice-Hall, 1970. 432 p.

> The editors themselves develop a conceptual framework for the comparative examination of the regions, or subordinate subsystems, of the world. The volume contains sixteen selections from the writings of prominent scholars on Western Europe, Latin America, Africa, and Southeast Asia, each of which is designed to illustrate and demonstrate the workability of the conceptualization and to analyze the nature of international politics within regions.

330 Cherry, E. Colin. WORLD COMMUNICATION: THREAT OR PROMISE: A SOCIO-TECHNICAL APPROACH. New York: Interscience Division, John Wiley and Sons, 1971. 229 p.

> An examination of the impact of new communications technologies on international relations. The author traces the evolution of communications capabilities from ancient times to the present, surveys the expansion of world communication since World War II, and assesses the impact of communications on nationalism and internationalism.

Integration and Alliance Theories

331 Cobb, Roger W., and Elder, Charles. INTERNATIONAL COMMUNITY: A REGIONAL AND GLOBAL STUDY. New York: Holt, Rinehart and Winston, 1970. 160 p.

The volume contains a survey of existing theories of integration and an assessment of areas of difference and overlap among scholars, together with a framework for analysis developed by the authors. The major portion of the study is devoted to the testing of propositions and the analysis of data on integration. Indicators of integration among fourteen North Atlantic countries over a twelve-year period between 1952 and 1964 are examined. The same indicators are applied to forty-nine countries throughout the world, for 1955 only, by use of multivariate techniques, primarily canonical correlational analysis.

332 Cox, Richard H., ed. THE STATE IN INTERNATIONAL RELATIONS. San Francisco: Chandler Publishing Co., 1965. 262 p.

A comprehensive collection drawing together forty-one writings, from the older and newer literature, on the nature of the state, sovereignty, integration into larger communities, and alternative political frameworks for the state: monarchy, republic, fascism, communism, and democracy.

333 Deutsch, Karl W., et al. INTERNATIONAL POLITICAL COMMUNITIES: AN ANTHOLOGY. Garden City, N.Y.: Anchor Books, 1966. 512 p.

A collection of fourteen writings representative of the literature on international integration of the 1950s and early 1960s. Among the topics examined are the dialectics of supranational unification; the Swiss pattern for a federated Europe; the Latin American Free Trade Association; East African economic integration; pan-Africanism; European unification; and political community in the North Atlantic area.

334 Deutsch, Karl W., et al. POLITICAL COMMUNITY AND THE NORTH ATLANTIC AREA. Princeton, N.J.: Princeton University Press, 1957. 228 p.

In an important study drawing upon the historical experience of nation building in the North Atlantic area, the authors study ten cases of integration and disintegration from which they draw inferences that may be applicable to the international level. From these historical experiences, the authors derive a series of propositions about communities based on features common to all or several of them. Depending upon the nature and extent of the integrative process, the newly formed units were classified as either "amalgamated" or "pluralistic" security communities.

335 Etzioni, Amitai. POLITICAL UNIFICATION. New York: Holt, Rinehart and Winston, 1965. 346 p.

Integration and Alliance Theories

Constructing a paradigm for the study of political unification, the author presents four case studies which examine the successes and failures of regional associations: the West Indies Federation, the European Economic Community, the United Arab Republic, and the Nordic Union. The study develops and tests propositions about political unification and sets forth a series of of tentative conclusions requiring further research.

336 Falk, Richard A., and Mendlowitz, Saul H. REGIONAL POLITICS AND WORLD ORDER. San Francisco: W.H. Freeman and Co., 1973. 475 p.

An anthology of recent writings focused on regionalism and the prospects for collaboration and integration at the international level. Included are selections dealing with theoretical approaches to the study of regional integration; the place of regional subsystems in alternative conceptions of the international system; the relationship between regionalism and globalism; the nature of interaction among states within a region; and the future prospects for regionalism.

337 Franck, Thomas M., ed. WHY FEDERATIONS FAIL: AN INQUIRY INTO THE REQUISITES FOR SUCCESSFUL FEDERALISM. New York: New York University Press, 1968. 212 p.

An examination of four unsuccessful examples of federalism: the West Indies, East Africa, Malaysia, and Rhodesia-Nyasaland. The authors assess the relative importance of such factors as constitutional division between the federal and local governments, culture, language, religion, leadership, and the distribution of resources in contributing to the success or failure of federations.

338 Friedman, Julian R., et al., eds. ALLIANCE IN INTERNATIONAL POLITICS. Boston: Allyn and Bacon, 1970. 383 p.

An anthology of twenty-one recent writings, theoretical and empirical, on alliances. Included are selections on such topics as bipolarity, multipolarity, and alliances; diplomatic coalitions and military alliances; alignments and realignments; stochastic models of war alliances; an economic theory of alliances; neutralists and neutralism; and the limits of international coalitions.

339 Friedrich, Carl J. EUROPE: AN EMERGENT NATION? New York: Harper and Row, 1969. 269 p.

After a good critique of studies of integration based on aggregate quantitative measures, the author analyzes in considerable detail the development of transnational relationships among industries and industrial associations, the agricultural community, labor unions, the academic community, and "grass-roots" integrative efforts in Western Europe. He concludes that Western

Integration and Alliance Theories

Europe, during the past generation, has experienced a rising level of integration among such groups, a phenomenon providing the basis for future momentum toward the unification of Europe.

340 Goodrich, Leland M., and Kay, David A., eds. INTERNATIONAL ORGANIZATION: POLITICS AND PROCESS. Madison: University of Wisconsin Press, 1973. 465 p.

An anthology of twenty-two writings, many of which are addressed to theoretical and conceptual problems of international integration. Included are selections on such topics as the study of bloc voting; international organization and the international system; transnational relations; and the integrative process in a regional and global context.

341 Groom, A.J.R., and Taylor, Paul, eds. THEORY AND PRACTICE IN INTERNATIONAL RELATIONS: FUNCTIONALISM. New York: Crane, Russak and Co., 1975. 354 p.

A collection of essays presenting contrasting analyses of functionalism as a theory of integration. Among the topics discussed by the sixteen contributors are neofunctional theories of regional integration; functionalism and strategies for international integration; functionalism and international organization; transnational associations; and functionalism and the resolution of international conflict.

342 Haas, Ernst B. BEYOND THE NATION-STATE: FUNCTIONALISM AND INTERNATIONAL ORGANIZATION. Stanford, Calif.: Stanford University Press, 1964. 595 p.

An important analysis and critique of the functionalist theory, together with a refinement of the author's conception of sector integration. A major portion of the volume is devoted to the testing of a theory of integration in a study of the International Labor Organization.

343 _____. TANGLE OF HOPES: AMERICAN COMMITMENTS AND WORLD ORDER. Englewood Cliffs, N.J.: Prentice-Hall, 1969. 306 p.

An analysis of the evolution of American policy toward and expectations from international organizations since World War II. The author assesses U.S. policies toward international organizations in dealing with problems of national security, alliances, arms control and disarmament, science and technology, economic and social development, international trade, aid, and investment. Included is an examination of the nature of interdependence in the world of the 1970s, together with an evaluation of the prospects for international organization in the years ahead.

344 _____. THE UNITING OF EUROPE: POLITICAL, SOCIAL AND ECONOMIC FORCES, 1950-1957. Stanford, Calif.: Stanford University Press, 1958. 552 p.

> A detailed examination of the European Coal and Steel Community in its formative years based on a conceptual framework for the study of international integration. In an elaboration of functionalist theory, the author hypothesizes the expansive logic of sector integration, namely, that successful integration in one sector "spills over" to other sectors. The study contains an assessment of the role of elite perceptions and expectations of joint reward as catalysts for integration. Detailed treatment is given to political parties, trade associations, labor unions and intergovernmental cooperation in an integrative process.

345 Hinsley, F.H. POWER AND THE PURSUIT OF PEACE: THEORY AND PRACTICE IN THE HISTORY OF RELATIONS BETWEEN STATES. New York: Cambridge University Press, 1967. 416 p.

> A history of proposals for peace and for international organization from the Middle Ages to the twentieth century. The author surveys the thought of such European writers as Rousseau, Kant, Bentham, and James Mill, and evaluates the Concert of Europe, the League of Nations, and the United Nations in a broad examination of the evolution of the modern international system.

346 Holsti, Ole R., et al. UNITY AND DISINTEGRATION IN INTERNATIONAL ALLIANCES. New York: John Wiley and Sons, 1973. 293 p.

> The authors subject older theories of alliance to empirical examination by means of rigorous and replicable techniques. Among the topics examined are national and international factors affecting alliances; the duration and disintegration of alliances; the effects of conflict and detente on alliance cohesion; and bloc-structure and intra-alliance conflict.

347 Jacob, Philip E., and Toscano, James V., eds. THE INTEGRATION OF POLITICAL COMMUNITIES. Philadelphia: J.B. Lippincott Co., 1964. 314 p.

> A collection of essays which examine conceptual and methodological problems in the development of a theory of political integration. Emphasis is placed on communications theory, transaction flows, values in political integration, and the learning of integrative habits. An effort is made to develop propositions relevant to the study of integration in a variety of settings from the urban to the international level.

348 Keohane, Robert O., and Nye, Joseph S., Jr., eds. TRANSNATIONAL RELATIONS AND WORLD POLITICS. Cambridge, Mass.: Harvard University Press, 1971. 428 p.

A series of essays focused on the need, as perceived by the authors, to find new approaches to the study of international organization and transnational relationships. Among the twenty chapters are analyses of transnational economic processes; labor organizations; the multinational corporation; private international finance; transnational networks in basic science; and the politics of transnational economic relations.

349 Lindberg, Leon N. THE POLITICAL DYNAMICS OF EUROPEAN ECONOMIC INTEGRATION. Stanford, Calif.: Stanford University Press, 1963. 367 p.

Developing a definition and conceptual framework of integration based on the shift of decision-making power from an national to supranational level, the author examines the integrative process in the European Community between 1959 and 1961.

350 Lindberg, Leon N., and Scheingold, Stuart A., eds. REGIONAL INTEGRATION: THEORY AND RESEARCH. Cambridge, Mass.: Harvard University Press, 1971. 427 p.

Students of integration theory survey the theory-building and methodological innovations of the 1960s and propose new areas for investigation. Among the topics examined are the utility of multivariate measurement in the study of political integration; neofunctionalism; international transactions and regional integration; and public opinion as an indicator of integration at the international level.

351 Liska, George. EUROPE ASCENDANT: THE INTERNATIONAL POLITICS OF UNIFICATION. Baltimore, Md.: Johns Hopkins Press, 1964. 182 p.

An analysis of the European unification process of the period following World War II in a broader historical and global perspective. The author reviews European unity efforts, sets forth conditions essential for the achievement of integration, and assesses the relationship between major forces shaping contemporary international politics and European unification.

352 _____. NATIONS IN ALLIANCE: THE LIMITS OF INTERDEPENDENCE. Baltimore, Md.: Johns Hopkins Press, 1962. 301 p.

The author analyzes the European state system in a study of the rationale for alignment, dealignment and realignment in international politics. In addition, the volume contains a major treatment of alliances in the postwar period, including their role and operation under conditions of bipolarity, the presence of non-aligned states, and emerging power centers.

Integration and Alliance Theories

353 Mitrany, David. A WORKING PEACE SYSTEM. Chicago: Quadrangle Books, 1966. 221 p.

> An analysis of international organization and alternative approaches--federal and functional--to integration among nations. As a leading proponent of functional integration, the author sets forth both a theory and strategy for its attainment and assesses the prospects for, and limitations of, regional and global organizations in the mid-twentieth century.

354 Neustadt, Richard E. ALLIANCE POLITICS. New York: Columbia University Press, 1970. 167 p.

> A good analysis of two major events in Anglo-American relations--the Suez crisis of 1956 and the cancellation by the United States of the Skybolt, an air-to-surface missile that Britain would have bought to extend the life of its manned aircraft strategic nuclear capability. The author utilizes a framework based on a bureaucratic model that treats policy decisions as the result of internal bargaining. According to the author, alliance politics is the product of the interaction of the internal bargaining process of national bureaucracies.

355 Nye, Joseph S., Jr. INTERNATIONAL REGIONALISM: READINGS. Boston: Little, Brown and Co., 1963. 432 p.

> A collection of essays on regionalism and world order, the prospects for federal and functional integration, regional organizations and the regulation of internal conflict, and patterns and catalysts making for regional integration. The volume contains writings on regionalism in Europe, Latin America, and Southeast Asia, as well as analyses of such organizations as the EEC, COMECON, the OAS, and the Regional Economic Commissions of the United Nations.

356 _____. PEACE IN PARTS: INTEGRATION AND CONFLICT IN REGIONAL ORGANIZATION. Boston: Little, Brown and Co., 1971. 210 p.

> Hypotheses are developed about regional integration with special emphasis on the refinement of neofunctionalist theory. Included are case studies, based on the author's model, dealing with integration and conflict resolution in the Organization of American States, the Organization of African Unity, and the Arab League.

357 Osgood, Robert E. ALLIANCES AND AMERICAN FOREIGN POLICY. Baltimore: Johns Hopkins University Press, 1968. 171 p.

> A useful examination of the changing nature and role of alliances since World War II, with emphasis on NATO and the

Integration and Alliance Theories

Warsaw Pact as well as alliances outside Europe. The author compares and contrasts the alliance system of the past generation with those of the eighteenth and nineteenth centuries, and assesses the implications of changing relationships for future American foreign policy.

358 Pentland, Charles. INTERNATIONAL THEORY AND EUROPEAN INTEGRATION. New York: Free Press, 1973. 283 p.

An examination of the pluralist, functionalist, neofunctionalist, and federalist approaches to integration, together with an analysis of their implications for an understanding of the European Community and its future prospects. The author assesses political integration as system-change, and sets forth requirements for a more powerful theory of integration.

359 Riker, William H. THE THEORY OF POLITICAL COALITIONS. New Haven, Conn.: Yale University Press, 1962. 300 p.

Making use of a mathematical model based on the theory of n-person games, the author develops an innovative theory of political coalitions with special emphasis on the size principle and side payments in determining the number of participants. Much of the volume is devoted to an analysis of coalitions in American politics and in international relations.

360 Russett, Bruce M. INTERNATIONAL REGIONS AND THE INTERNATIONAL SYSTEM: A STUDY IN POLITICAL ECOLOGY. Chicago: Rand McNally and Co., 1967. 252 p.

An effort to develop and utilize a methodology based on factor analysis to study regionalism. Using data about such dimensions as levels of literacy, membership, and voting behavior in international organizations, trade patterns, economic development, per capita GNP, transnational communications, and population density, the author delineates regions based on homogeneity among nations in a large number of the dimensions studied. Included are discussions of regionalism and integration, and the implications of regional integration for the creation of a world community.

Chapter 9

MAJOR INTERNATIONAL RELATIONS JOURNALS

Numerous and diverse scholarly journals, many published in the United States, contribute to the extensive literature of international relations. The following listing of major journals reflects the vast scope of the discipline as well as the richness and diversity of approach to the study of international relations. Excluded from this list are the many excellent journals devoted exclusively or largely to area studies, as well as publications in languages other than English.

ABC POL. SCI.: ADVANCE BIBLIOGRAPHY OF CONTENTS: POLITICAL SCIENCE AND GOVERNMENT. Santa Barbara, Calif.: American Bibliographic Press, CLIO Press, 1971-- . 9 editions annually.

> This publication reprints the contents of major journals in political science and international relations published in the United States and abroad. It provides an index of current periodical literature on all aspects of international relations.

AMERICAN BEHAVIORAL SCIENTIST. Beverly Hills, Calif.: Sage Publications, 1956-- . Quarterly.

> A journal focused on the application of innovative methodologies to the study of the social sciences. Each issue contains articles devoted to a special topic, some of which are of direct interest to the student of international relations.

AMERICAN POLITICAL SCIENCE REVIEW. Washington, D.C.: American Political Science Association, 1906-- . Quarterly.

> Published by the American Political Science Association, the journal frequently contains articles and research notes on international studies addressed to theoretical and methodological problems and innovations. A substantial portion of the REVIEW is devoted to reviews of books on all aspects of the study of international relations.

ANNALS OF THE AMERICAN ACADEMY OF POLITICAL AND SOCIAL SCIENCE. Philadelphia, Pa.: The American Academy of Political and Social Science, 1904-- . Bimonthly.

International Relations Journals

Published six times a year with each issue focused on a general topic of current interest, sometimes dealing with international relations research as well as substantive problems of foreign policy. Each issue contains a large section of book reviews on all aspects of political science and international relations.

BRITISH JOURNAL OF INTERNATIONAL STUDIES. Edinburgh, Scotland: Aberdeen University Press, 1975-- . Quarterly.

The journal of the British International Studies Association, designed to present a wide variety of methodological approaches and to encourage debate on both substantive and procedural aspects of international relations. In addition, each issue contains review articles surveying the literature in a particular field.

COMPARATIVE POLITICS. New York: City University of New York, 1967-- . Quarterly.

A journal that publishes articles based on innovative methodologies, frequently quantitative, on comparative aspects of international studies and political science. Included are review articles and research notes.

COOPERATION AND CONFLICT: NORDIC JOURNAL OF INTERNATIONAL POLITICS. Oslo, Norway: Univerisitetsforlaget, 1965-- . Quarterly.

A journal devoted to the publication of manuscripts dealing with substantive policy issues as well as theory and research based on new methodologies in international affairs. Each issue contains a short book review section.

FOREIGN AFFAIRS. New York: Council on Foreign Relations, 1922-- . Quarterly.

A leading journal containing analyses of contemporary international issues, published by the Council on Foreign Relations. Included are articles on all aspects of foreign policy and international security by contributors from the United States and abroad. Each issue includes a useful list of new books and monographs in international affairs.

FOREIGN POLICY. New York: National Affairs, 1970-- . Quarterly.

A journal devoted to analyses of current foreign policy problems, often presenting opposing points of view and perspectives. While containing articles on military security, a large number of the contributors deal with economic and resource issues, as well as other problems currently facing, or likely to face, American foreign policy.

International Relations Journals

INTERNATIONAL AFFAIRS. London: Oxford University Press, 1922-- .
Quarterly.

>The journal of the Royal Institute of International Affairs in London containing articles on theoretical as well as policy problems in international relations written by scholars and policymakers from Britain as well as other countries. A major portion of the journal is devoted to reviews of recently published books on all aspects of international affairs.

INTERNATIONAL AFFAIRS (Moscow). Chekhov, Moscow Region: Chekhov Printing Works, 1954-- . Monthly.

>A monthly journal containing Soviet analyses of current international problems and communist perspectives on the nature of the international system and the foreign policies of the Soviet Union and other countries.

INTERNATIONAL JOURNAL. Toronto: Canadian Institute of International Affairs, 1945-- . Quarterly.

>A Canadian quarterly devoted to the publication of manuscripts by authors from many countries on theory and the policy-oriented problems of international studies. Occasionally, the JOURNAL publishes special issues devoted to such topics as problems of theory building and the nature of the international system. Included in each issue are reviews of new books.

INTERNATIONAL ORGANIZATION. Boston: World Peace Foundation, 1948-- .
Quarterly.

>A journal containing articles not only on theoretical, methodological, and substantive problems of the study of international organization, but also on other issues of world politics and public policy. Included are research notes, review essays of current literature, and bibliographies of recent writings.

INTERNATIONAL POLITICAL SCIENCE ABSTRACTS. Paris: International Political Science Association, 1950-- . Bimonthly.

>Published bimonthly by the International Political Science Association in cooperation with the International Committee for Social Sciences Documentation. Contains listings and abstracts of recently published books and articles by scholars in the United States and abroad dealing with international relations and political studies within nations.

INTERNATIONAL SOCIAL SCIENCE JOURNAL. Paris: UNESCO, 1948-- .
Quarterly.

>Published by the United Nations Educational, Scientific, and Cultural Organization (UNESCO), with each issue devoted to

International Relations Journals

a special topic of current international interest, such as development studies, the social assessment of technology, and population policy. Included in each issue is a section on United Nations documentation, as well as new books.

INTERNATIONAL STUDIES QUARTERLY. Beverly Hills, Calif.: Sage Publications, 1957-- . Quarterly.

> The publication of the International Studies Association devoted largely to articles on theory and methodology, with special, but not exclusive, emphasis on quantification. Emphasizing an interdisciplinary approach, the journal contains contributions on a wide range of topics.

JOURNAL OF CONFLICT RESOLUTION. Beverly Hills, Calif.: Sage Publications, 1956-- . Quarterly.

> An interdisciplinary journal devoted to the presentation of research on international and intergroup conflict, within and among nations. The emphasis is on contributions containing innovative methodologies applied to conflict studies. Contains review articles and notes on basic research of interest to scholars in several disciplines.

JOURNAL OF INTERNATIONAL AFFAIRS. New York: Columbia University Press, 1946-- . Biannual.

> Published twice a year by the School of International Affairs, Columbia University. Devoted to the publication of articles on theory as well as substantive aspects of international relations. Contains an extensive listing of new books divided into each of the major categories, or subdivisions, of international studies, and on a regional, and country, basis.

THE JOURNAL OF SOCIAL AND POLITICAL AFFAIRS. Washington, D.C.: Council on American Affairs, 1976-- . Quarterly.

> A new journal whose goal is to encourage research and present the findings of psychologists, political scientists and other social scientists on problems of the group, community, nation, and relations among peoples. Issues of the JOURNAL will contain articles of interest to the student of international relations.

LO SPETTATORE INTERNAZIONALE. Rome: Instituto Affari Internazionali, 1965-- . Quarterly.

> Published in English and Italian by the Instituto Affari Internazionali in Rome, the journal contains articles on such topics as Italian foreign policy, European integration, and the nature of the international system. It also provides a summary of activities of the Instituto Affari Internazionali.

International Relations Journals

ORBIS. Philadelphia, Pa.: Foreign Policy Research Institute, 1956-- . Quarterly.

> Contains articles by scholars and policymakers on all aspects of world affairs, including theory, strategy, foreign policy, and economic issues as they involve international relations. Occasionally, issues are devoted to a special topic of current importance. Each issue contains a book review section and an annotated listing of new books and monographs.

PEACE RESEARCH ABSTRACTS JOURNAL. Oakville, Ontario: Canadian Peace Research Institute, 1963-- . Monthly.

> Published monthly by the Canadian Peace Research Institute in order to provide summaries of articles and books on substantive issues of current importance, but also research and theory building efforts in such areas as decision making and communications, game theory, operations research, prediction, and simulation studies in international relations.

POLITICAL SCIENCE QUARTERLY. New York: Academy of Political Science, 1886-- . Quarterly.

> Published by the Academy of Political Science and edited by the political science faculty of Columbia University, this journal frequently contains articles on international relations, based on nonquantitative approaches and methodologies. A major section of each issue contains book reviews.

POLITICAL STUDIES. Oxford, Eng.: Clarendon Press, 1952-- . Quarterly.

> Published by the Political Studies Association of the United Kingdom, this journal frequently publishes articles of immediate relevance to the student of international relations interested in theoretical, conceptual, and methodological problems. Included in each issue is a book review section.

WORLD AFFAIRS: A QUARTERLY REVIEW OF INTERNATIONAL PROBLEMS. Washington, D.C.: American Peace Society, (Commenced 1834 as the ADVOCATE OF PEACE, renamed WORLD AFFAIRS in 1932). Quarterly.

> Published by the American Peace Society, the journal contains articles on American foreign policy as well as on international organization and national security affairs. Each issue contains several reviews of new books.

WORLD POLITICS. Princeton, N.J.: Princeton University Press, Center for International Studies, 1957-- . Quarterly.

> A journal containing articles on theory and methodology, and also on substantive issues such as political development, foreign policy, and arms control. Each issue contains review articles dealing with one or more books of current scholarly interest.

Chapter 10
RECOMMENDED BOOKS FOR SMALL OR PERSONAL LIBRARIES

Allison, Graham T. ESSENCE OF DECISION: EXPLAINING THE CUBAN MISSILE CRISIS. Boston: Little, Brown and Co., 1971. (No. 120).

Ardrey, Robert. THE TERRITORIAL IMPERATIVE: A PERSONAL INQUIRY INTO THE ANIMAL ORIGINS OF PROPERTY AND NATIONS. New York: Atheneum, 1966. (No. 273).

Aron, Raymond. ON WAR. W.W. Norton & Co., 1968. (No. 209).

_____. PEACE AND WAR: A THEORY OF INTERNATIONAL RELATIONS. Garden City, N.Y.: Doubleday and Co., 1966. (No. 73).

Beard, Charles A. THE IDEA OF NATIONAL INTEREST: AN ANALYTICAL STUDY IN AMERICAN FOREIGN POLICY. New York: Macmillan Co., 1934. (No. 122).

Beaufre, André. DETERRENCE AND STRATEGY. New York: Frederick A. Praeger, 1966. (No. 210).

Boulding, Kenneth E. CONFLICT AND DEFENSE: A GENERAL THEORY. New York: Harper and Row, 1962. (No. 213).

Bozeman, Adda B. POLITICS AND CULTURE IN INTERNATIONAL HISTORY. Princeton, N.J.: Princeton University Press, 1960. (No. 77).

Brodie, Bernard. STRATEGY IN THE MISSILE AGE. Princeton, N.J.: Princeton University Press, 1965. (No. 214).

_____. WAR AND POLITICS. New York: Macmillan Co., 1973. (No. 215).

Recommended Books

Brzezinski, Zbigniew. BETWEEN TWO AGES: AMERICA'S ROLE IN THE TECHNETRONIC ERA. New York: Viking Press, 1970. (No. 177).

Bull, Hedley. THE CONTROL OF THE ARMS RACE: DISARMAMENT AND ARMS CONTROL IN THE MISSILE AGE. New York: Frederick A. Praeger, 1961. (No. 218).

Cantori, Louis J., and Spiegel, Steven L., eds. THE INTERNATIONAL POLITICS OF REGIONS: A COMPARATIVE APPROACH. Englewood Cliffs, N.J.: Prentice-Hall, 1970. (No. 329).

Carr, E.H. THE TWENTY YEARS' CRISIS, 1919-1939: AN INTRODUCTION TO THE STUDY OF INTERNATIONAL RELATIONS. New York: St. Martin's Press, 1962. First published in 1939 by Macmillan, London and St. Martin's Press. (No. 8).

Choucri, Nazli, and North, Robert C. NATIONS IN CONFLICT: NATIONAL GROWTH AND INTERNATIONAL VIOLENCE. San Francisco: W.H. Freeman and and Co., 1975. (No. 281).

Claude, Inis L., Jr. POWER AND INTERNATIONAL RELATIONS. New York: Random House, 1962. (No. 179).

Cohen, Benjamin J. THE QUESTION OF IMPERIALISM: THE POLITICAL ECONOMY OF DOMINANCE AND DEPENDENCE. New York: Basic Books, 1973. (No. 282).

Cook, Thomas I., and Moos, Malcolm. POWER THROUGH PURPOSE: THE REALISM OF IDEALISM AS A BASIS FOR FOREIGN POLICY. Baltimore, Md.: Johns Hopkins Press, 1954. (No. 126).

Coplin, William D., and Kegley, Charles W., Jr., eds. ANALYZING INTERNATIONAL RELATIONS: A MULTIMETHOD INTRODUCTION. New York: Frederick A. Praeger, 1975. (No. 11).

Coser, Lewis A. THE FUNCTIONS OF SOCIAL CONFLICT. New York: Free Press, 1956. (No. 284).

Crosier, Brian. A THEORY OF CONFLICT. New York: Charles Scribner's Sons, 1974. (No. 285).

Deutsch, Karl W. THE ANALYSIS OF INTERNATIONAL RELATIONS. Englewood Cliffs, N.J.: Prentice-Hall, 1968. (No. 12).

Deutsch, Karl W., et al. POLITICAL COMMUNITY AND THE NORTH ATLANTIC AREA. Princeton, N.J.: Princeton University Press, 1957. (No. 334).

Recommended Books

Dougherty, James E., and Pfaltzgraff, Robert L., Jr. CONTENDING THEORIES OF INTERNATIONAL RELATIONS. Philadelphia: J.B. Lippincott Co., 1971. (No. 13).

Earle, Edward Meade, ed. MAKERS OF MODERN STRATEGY: MILITARY THOUGHT FROM MACHIAVELLI TO HITLER. New York: Atheneum, 1970. (No. 222).

Eckstein, Harry, ed. INTERNAL WAR: PROBLEMS AND APPROACHES. New York: Free Press of Glencoe, 1964. (No. 288).

Emerson, Rupert. FROM EMPIRE TO NATION: THE RISE TO SELF-ASSERTION OF ASIAN AND AFRICAN PEOPLES. Boston: Beacon Press, 1960. (No. 82).

Etzioni, Amitai. POLITICAL UNIFICATION. New York: Holt, Rinehart and Winston, 1965. (No. 335).

Falk, Richard A. A STUDY OF FUTURE WORLDS. New York: Free Press, 1975. (No. 83).

Fox, William T.R. THE AMERICAN STUDY OF INTERNATIONAL RELATIONS. Columbia: University of South Carolina Press, 1968. (No. 20).

Friedman, Julian R., et al., eds. ALLIANCE IN INTERNATIONAL POLITICS. Boston: Allyn and Bacon, 1970. (No. 338).

Friedrich, Carl J. EUROPE: AN EMERGENT NATION? New York: Harper and Row, 1969. (No. 339).

Gallois, Pierre. THE BALANCE OF TERROR: STRATEGY FOR THE NUCLEAR AGE. Boston: Houghton Mifflin Co., 1961. (No. 223).

George, Alexander L., and Smoke, Richard. DETERRENCE IN AMERICAN FOREIGN POLICY: THEORY AND PRACTICE. New York: Columbia University Press, 1974. (No. 225).

Guetzkow, Harold, et al. SIMULATION IN INTERNATIONAL RELATIONS: DEVELOPMENTS FOR RESEARCH AND TEACHING. Englewood Cliffs, N.J.: Prentice-Hall, 1963. (No. 22).

Gulick, Edward V. EUROPE'S CLASSICAL BALANCE OF POWER. Ithaca, N.Y.: Cornell University Press, 1955. (No. 189).

Gurr, Ted Robert. WHY MEN REBEL. Princeton, N.J.: Princeton University Press, 1970. (No. 293).

Recommended Books

Haas, Ernst B. BEYOND THE NATION-STATE: FUNCTIONALISM AND INTERNATIONAL ORGANIZATION. Stanford, Calif.: Stanford University Press, 1964. (No. 342).

_____. THE UNITING OF EUROPE: POLITICAL, SOCIAL AND ECONOMIC FORCES, 1950-1957. Stanford, Calif.: Stanford University Press, 1958. (No. 344).

Halperin, Morton H. BUREAUCRATIC POLITICS AND FOREIGN POLICY. Washington, D.C.: Brookings Institution, 1974. (No. 130).

Hermann, Charles F. CRISES IN FOREIGN POLICY: A SIMULATION ANALSIS. Indianapolis and New York: The Bobbs-Merrill Co., 1969. (No. 134).

Hitch, Charles J., and McKean, Roland N. THE ECONOMICS OF DEFENSE IN THE NUCLEAR AGE. Cambridge, Mass.: Harvard University Press, 1963. (No. 233).

Hobson, J.A. IMPERIALISM: A STUDY. 3d ed. London: George Allen & Unwin, 1948. (No. 294).

Hoffmann, Stanley. THE STATE OF WAR: ESSAYS IN THE THEORY AND PRACTICE OF INTERNATIONAL POLITICS. New York: Frederick A. Praeger, 1965. (No. 28).

_____, ed. CONTEMPORARY THEORY IN INTERNATIONAL RELATIONS. Englewood Cliffs, N.J.: Prentice-Hall, 1960. (No. 29).

Holsti, Ole R. CRISIS, ESCALATION, WAR. Montreal: McGill-Queen's University Press, 1972. (No. 295).

Iklé, Fred Charles. HOW NATIONS NEGOTIATE. New York: Harper and Row, 1964. (No. 136).

Jervis, Robert. THE LOGIC OF IMAGES IN INTERNATIONAL RELATIONS. Princeton, N.J.: Princeton University Press, 1970. (No. 296).

Kahn, Herman. ON THERMONUCLEAR WAR. Princeton, N.J.: Princeton University Press, 1961. (No. 237).

Kaplan, Morton A. SYSTEM AND PROCESS IN INTERNATIONAL RELATIONS. New York: John Wiley and Sons, 1957. (No. 94).

_____, NEW APPROACHES TO INTERNATIONAL RELATIONS. New York: St. Martin's Press, 1968. (No. 30).

Recommended Books

Kegley, Charles W., Jr., et al., eds. INTERNATIONAL EVENTS AND THE COMPARATIVE ANALYSIS OF FOREIGN POLICY. Columbia: University of South Carolina Press, 1975. (No. 139).

Kemp, Geoffrey, et al., eds. THE SUPERPOWERS IN A MULTINUCLEAR WORLD. Lexington, Mass.: D.C. Heath and Co., 1974. (No. 240).

Kennan, George F. AMERICAN DIPLOMACY, 1900-1950. New York: Mentor Books, 1951. (No. 140).

Keynes, John Maynard. THE ECONOMIC CONSEQUENCES OF THE PEACE. New York: Harcourt, Brace and Howe, 1920. (No. 299).

Kindleberger, Charles P. POWER AND MONEY: THE POLITICS OF INTERNATIONAL ECONOMICS AND THE ECONOMICS OF INTERNATIONAL POLITICS. New York: Basic Books, 1970. (No. 31).

Kintner, William R., and Pfaltzgraff, Robert L., Jr., eds. SALT: IMPLICATIONS FOR ARMS CONTROL IN THE 1970'S. Pittsburgh: University of Pittsburgh Press, 1973. (No. 242).

Kissinger, Henry A. AMERICAN FOREIGN POLICY. Enl. ed. New York: W.W. Norton and Co., 1974. (No. 141).

_____. A WORLD RESTORED: THE POLITICS OF CONSERVATISM IN A REVOLUTIONARY AGE. New York: Grosset and Dunlap, 1964. (No. 95).

_____. NUCLEAR WEAPONS AND FOREIGN POLICY. New York: Harper and Brothers for the Council on Foreign Relations, 1957. (No. 244).

Klineberg, Otto. THE HUMAN DIMENSION IN INTERNATIONAL RELATIONS. New York: Holt, Rinehart and Winston, 1964. (No. 300).

Knorr, Klaus. MILITARY POWER AND POTENTIAL. Lexington, Mass.: D.C. Heath and Co., 1970. (No. 246).

Knorr, Klaus and Rosenau, James N., eds. CONTENDING APPROACHES TO INTERNATIONAL POLITICS. Princeton, N.J.: Princeton University Press, 1969. (No. 32).

Kohn, Hans. THE IDEA OF NATIONALISM: A STUDY OF ITS ORIGINS AND BACKGROUND. New York: Macmillan Co., 1960. (No. 97).

Recommended Books

Lasswell, Harold D. WORLD POLITICS AND PERSONAL INSECURITY. New York: Free Press, 1965. (No. 301).

Lenin, V.I. IMPERIALISM: THE HIGHEST STAGE OF CAPITALISM. New York: International Publishers, 1939. (No. 302).

———. STATE AND REVOLUTION. New York: International Publishers, 1932. (No. 303).

Lerche, Charles O., Jr., and Said, Abdul A. CONCEPTS OF INTERNATIONAL POLITICS. Englewood Cliffs, N.J.: Prentice-Hall, 1964. (No. 35).

Lindberg, Leon N., and Scheingold, Stuart A., eds. REGIONAL INTEGRATION: THEORY AND RESEARCH. Cambridge, Mass.: Harvard University Press, 1971. (No. 350).

Liska, George. NATIONS IN ALLIANCE: THE LIMITS OF INTERDEPENDENCE. Baltimore, Md.: Johns Hopkins Press, 1962. (No. 352).

Lorenz, Konrad. ON AGGRESSION. New York: Harcourt, Brace and World, 1963. (No. 305).

McClelland, Charles A. THEORY AND THE INTERNATIONAL SYSTEM. New York: Macmillan Co., 1966. (No. 37).

McGowan, Patrick J., ed. SAGE INTERNATIONAL YEARBOOK OF FOREIGN POLICY STUDIES. Vol. 1. Beverly Hills, Calif.: Sage Publications, 1973. (No. 145).

———, ed. SAGE INTERNATIONAL YEARBOOK OF FOREIGN POLICY STUDIES. Vol. 2. Beverly Hills, Calif.: Sage Publications, 1974. (No. 146).

Mackinder, Sir Halford J. DEMOCRATIC IDEALS AND REALITY. New York: W.W. Norton and Co., 1962. (No. 192).

Mahan, Alfred Thayer. THE INFLUENCE OF SEA POWER UPON HISTORY, 1600-1783. 2d ed. London: Methuen and Co., 1964. (No. 193).

Mao Tse-tung. ON GUERRILLA WARFARE. Translated by Samuel B. Griffith. New York: Frederick A. Praeger, 1961. (No. 250).

Mitrany, David. A WORKING PEACE SYSTEM. Chicago: Quadrangle Books, 1966. (No. 353).

Recommended Books

Morgenstern, Oskar. THE QUESTION OF NATIONAL DEFENSE. New York: Random House, 1959. (No. 251).

Morgenthau, Hans J. IN DEFENSE OF THE NATIONAL INTEREST: A CRITICAL EXAMINATION OF AMERICAN FOREIGN POLICY. New York: Alfred A. Knopf, 1951. (No. 150).

_____. POLITICS AMONG NATIONS: THE STRUGGLE FOR POWER AND PEACE. 5th ed. New York: Alfred A. Knopf, 1973. (No. 106).

Neustadt, Richard E. ALLIANCE POLITICS. New York: Columbia University Press, 1970. (No. 354).

Nicolson, Harold. DIPLOMACY. 2d ed. London: Oxford University Press, 1958. (No. 154).

Niebuhr, Reinhold. THE STRUCTURE OF NATIONS AND EMPIRES. New York: Charles Scribner's Sons, 1959. (No. 107).

Nye, Joseph S., Jr. PEACE IN PARTS: INTEGRATION AND CONFLICT IN REGIONAL ORGANIZATION. Boston: Little, Brown and Co., 1971. (No. 356).

Osgood, Robert E. IDEALS AND SELF-INTEREST IN AMERICA'S FOREIGN RELATIONS: THE GREAT TRANSFORMATION OF THE TWENTIETH CENTURY. Chicago: University of Chicago Press, 1953. (No. 158).

Paige, Glenn D. THE KOREAN DECISION: JUNE 24-30, 1950. New York: Free Press, 1968. (No. 159).

Pfaltzgraff, Robert L., Jr., ed. POLITICS AND THE INTERNATIONAL SYSTEM. 2d ed. Philadelphia: J.B. Lippincott Co., 1972. (No. 111).

Pruitt, Dean G., and Snyder, Richard D. THEORY AND RESEARCH ON THE CAUSES OF WAR. Englewood Cliffs, N.J.: Prentice-Hall, 1969. (No. 46).

Riker, William H. THE THEORY OF POLITICAL COALITIONS. New Haven: Yale University Press, 1962. (No. 359).

Rosenau, James N., ed. COMPARING FOREIGN POLICIES: THEORIES, FINDINGS, AND METHODS. New York: Halsted Press Division, John Wiley and Sons, 1974; Sage Publications. (No. 161).

_____, ed. DOMESTIC SOURCES OF FOREIGN POLICY. New York: Free Press, 1967. (No. 162).

Recommended Books

_____, ed. INTERNATIONAL POLITICS AND FOREIGN POLICY: A READER IN RESEARCH AND THEORY. Rev. ed. New York: Free Press, 1969. (No. 53).

_____, ed. LINKAGE POLITICS: ESSAYS ON THE CONVERGENCE OF NATIONAL AND INTERNATIONAL SYSTEMS. New York: Free Press, 1969. (No. 163).

_____, ed. THE SCIENTIFIC STUDY OF FOREIGN POLICY. New York: Free Press, 1971. (No. 164).

Rummel, R.J. THE DIMENSIONS OF NATIONS. Beverly Hills, Calif.: Sage Publications, 1972. (No. 166).

Russett, Bruce M., ed. ECONOMIC THEORIES OF INTERNATIONAL POLITICS. Chicago: Markham Publishing Co., 1968. (No. 316).

Russett, Bruce M., et al. WORLD HANDBOOK OF POLITICAL AND SOCIAL INDICATORS. New Haven: Yale University Press, 1964. (No. 113).

Schelling, Thomas C. THE STRATEGY OF CONFLICT. New York: Oxford University Press, 1963. (No. 260).

Shubik, Martin, ed. GAME THEORY AND RELATED APPROACHES TO SOCIAL BEHAVIOR: SELECTIONS. New York: John Wiley and Sons, 1964. (No. 59).

Singer, J. David, ed. QUANTITATIVE INTERNATIONAL POLITICS. New York: Free Press, 1968. (No. 61).

Snyder, Richard C., et al., eds. FOREIGN POLICY DECISION-MAKING: AN APPROACH TO THE STUDY OF INTERNATIONAL POLITICS. New York: Free Press of Glencoe, 1962. (No. 169).

Sokolovskiy, V.D. SOVIET MILITARY STRATEGY. Edited by Harriet Fast Scott. 3d ed. New York: Crane, Russak & Co., 1975. (No. 263).

Sprout, Harold, and Sprout, Margaret. THE ECOLOGICAL PERSPECTIVE ON HUMAN AFFAIRS WITH SPECIAL REFERENCE TO INTERNATIONAL POLITICS. Princeton, N.J.: Princeton University Press, 1965. (No. 200).

Spykman, Nicholas J. AMERICA'S STRATEGY IN WORLD POLITICS: THE UNITED STATES AND THE BALANCE OF POWER. New York: Harcourt, Brace and Co., 1942. (No. 201).

Recommended Books

Strausz-Hupé, Robert. GEOPOLITICS: THE STRUGGLE FOR SPACE AND POWER. New York: G.P. Putnam's Sons, 1942. (No. 204).

Strausz-Hupé, Robert, et al. PROTRACTED CONFLICT. New York: Harper and Row, 1963. (No. 267).

Tanter, Raymond, and Ullman, Richard H., eds. THEORY AND POLICY IN INTERNATIONAL RELATIONS. Princeton University Press, 1972. (No. 63).

Thompson, Kenneth W. POLITICAL REALISM AND THE CRISIS OF WORLD POLITICS: AN AMERICAN APPROACH TO FOREIGN POLICY. Princeton, N.J.: Princeton University Press, 1960. (No. 64).

Von Clausewitz, Carl. ON WAR. London: Kegan Paul, Trench, Truehmer and Co., 1911. (No. 269).

Waltz, Kenneth N. MAN, THE STATE, AND WAR: A THEORETICAL ANALYSIS. New York: Columbia University Press, 1959. (No. 325).

Wilkenfeld, Jonathan, ed. CONFLICT BEHAVIOR AND LINKAGE POLITICS. New York: David McKay Co., 1973. (No. 326).

Wolfers, Arnold. DISCORD AND COLLABORATION: ESSAYS ON INTERNATIONAL POLITICS. Baltimore: Johns Hopkins Press, 1962. (No. 67).

Wright, Quincy. THE STUDY OF INTERNATIONAL RELATIONS. New York: Appleton-Century-Crofts, 1955. (No. 68).

_____. A STUDY OF WAR. 2d ed. Chicago: University of Chicago Press, 1965. (No. 327).

Zawodny, J.K., ed. MAN AND INTERNATIONAL RELATIONS. 2 vols. San Francisco: Chandler Publishing Co., 1967. (No. 70).

AUTHOR INDEX

This index includes authors, editors, compilers, and contributors. References are to entry numbers, unless the number is preceded by a "p." (to indicate reference is to a page number). Alphabetization is letter by letter.

A

Ake, Claude 328
Allison, Graham T. 120, p. 119
Angell, Norman 207
Ardrey, Robert 273, p. 119
Arendt, Hannah 72, 274
Aron, Raymond 73, 208-9, p. 119
Axline, W. Andrew 74

B

Bailey, Thomas A. 121
Banks, Arthur S. 1
Barnett, Robert W. p. 68
Beard, Charles A. 122, p. 119
Beaufre, André 210, p. 119
Beitz, Charles R. 275
Bell, Daniel 75
Ben-Dak, Joseph D. 276
Bennett, John C. 211
Berle, Adolf A. 175
Black, Cyril E. 76
Blainey, Geoffrey 277
Bloomfield, Lincoln 278
Bobrow, Davis B. 2-3, 212
Boulding, Kenneth E. 213, 258, 279, p. 119
Bowie, Robert R. 245
Bozeman, Adda B. 77, p. 119
Brennan, Donald G. 258

Brodie, Bernard 118, 214-16, 245, p. 119
Brodie, Fawn M. 216
Brown, Neville 217
Brucan, Silviu 176
Bruce-Biggs, B. 93
Brzezinski, Zbigniew 177, p. 120
Buchan, Alastair 78, 178, 245
Buell, Raymond Leslie 4
Bull, Hedley p. 6, 218, p. 120
Burke, William T. 266
Burton, J.W. 5-7
Butterfield, Herbert 123

C

Cantori, Louis J. 329, p. 120
Cantril, Hadley 280
Cardozo, Michael A. 266
Carr, E.H. p. 2, 8, 79, p. 57, p. 120
Chammah, Albert M. 49
Cherry, E. Colin 330
Choucri, Nazli 118, 281, p. 120
Clark, Eric 124
Claude, Inis L., Jr. 179, p. 120
Cobb, Roger W. 331
Cohen, Benjamin J. 282, p. 120
Cohen, Bernard C. 125
Cohen, Saul B. 180
Collins, John M. 219

Author Index

Cook, Thomas I. 126, p. 120
Coplin, William D. 9-11, 118, 156, p. 120
Coser, Lewis A. 283-84, p. 120
Cox, Kevin R. 181
Cox, Richard H. 332
Crabb, Cecil V., Jr. 80
Crosier, Brian 285, p. 120

D

Davies, James Chowning 286
Davison, W. Phillips 127
Debray, Régis 220
DeJouvenel, Bertrand 182
De la Blache, Vidal 183
de Rivera, Joseph H. 128
Deutsch, Karl W. 12, p. 28, 81, 333-34, p. 120
Dinerstein, Herbert S. 118, 221
Dollard, John p. 85
Donelan, M.D. 311
Doob, Leonard W. p. 85
Dorpalen, Andreas 184
Dougherty, James E. 13, p. 121
Duchacek, Ivo D. 14
Dunn, Frederick Sherwood 287
Duroselle, Jean-Baptiste 50

E

Earle, Edward Meade 222, p. 121
Eckstein, Harry 288, p. 121
Elder, Charles 331
Emeny, Brooks 185, 319
Emerson, Rupert 82, p. 121
Enthoven, Alan 245
Etzioni, Amitai 335, p. 121
Eubank, Keith 129

F

Fairgrieve, James 186
Falk, Richard A. 83, 266, 336, p. 121
Farrell, John C. 15
Farrell, R. Barry 16
Ferkiss, Victor 187
Finkelstein, Lawrence S. 188
Finkelstein, Marina S. 188

Finlay, David J. 17, 289
Fisher, Roger 266, 290-91
Fliess, Peter J. 84
Forsyth, M.G. 18
Forward, Nigel 19
Fox, William T.R. 20-21, p. 121
Franck, Thomas M. 337
Frankel, Joseph 130
Fried, Morton 292
Friedman, Julian R. 338, p. 121
Friedrich, Carl J. 339, p. 121

G

Gabor, Dennis 85
Gallois, Pierre p. 68, 223, 245, p. 121
Gardner, Richard N. 258
Gareau, Frederick H. 224
George, Alexander L. 225, p. 121
Goodrich, Leland M. 340
Goodwin, Geoffrey L. 86
Gray, Richard B. 226
Green, Philip 227
Griffith, Samuel B. 250, p. 124
Groom, A.J.R. 341
Guetzkow, Harold 22, p. 121
Gulick, Edward V. 189, p. 121
Gurr, Ted Robert 293, p. 121

H

Haas, Ernst B. p. 4, p. 102, 342-44, p. 122
Haas, Michael 23
Halperin, Morton H. 131, 228-30, p. 122
Harkabi, Y. 231
Harr, John Ensor 132
Harrison, Horace V. 24
Hartmann, Frederick H. 25
Hauser, Philip M. 190
Hayter, William 133
Hazard, Harry W. 116
Hekhius, Dale J. 87
Herman, Theodore 275
Hermann, Charles F. 26, 134, p. 122
Herz, John H. 27, 88
Hinsley, F.H. 345
Hitch, Charles J. 232-33, p. 122

Author Index

Hoag, Malcolm W. 258
Hobson, J.A. 294, p. 122
Ho Chi Minh 234
Hoffmann, Stanley 28-29, p. 122
Hollick, Ann L. 135
Holsti, K.J. 89
Holsti, Ole R. 295, 346, p. 122
Hovet, Thomas, Jr. 17
Huntington, Ellsworth p. 3, 90-91
Huntington, Samuel P. 235, 245

I

Iklé, Fred Charles 136, p. 68, p. 122
Inglehart, Ronald p. 102

J

Jacob, Philip E. 347
Jacobson, Harold Karan 137
James, Alan 92
Jervis, Robert 296, p. 122
Johnson, Chalmers 297
Johnson, E.A. 138

K

Kahn, Herman 93, 236-38, 245, p. 122
Kaplan, Morton A. 30, p. 27, 94, 239, 258, p. 122
Kay, David A. 340
Kegley, Charles W., Jr. 11, 139, p. 120, p. 123
Kelman, Herbert C. 298
Kemp, Geoffrey 240, p. 123
Kennan, George F. p. 4, 140, p. 123
Keohane, Robert O. 348
Keynes, John Maynard 299, p. 123
Kindleberger, Charles P. 31, p. 123
Kintner, William R. 241-43, p. 123
Kissinger, Henry A. pp. 4-5, 95, 141, 244-45, p. 123
Klineberg, Otto 300, p. 123
Knorr, Klaus p. 6, p. 7, 32-33, 191, 246, p. 123
Kohn, Hans p. 3, 96-97, p. 123

Kothari, Rajni 98
Kriesberg, Louis 34

L

Lall, Arthur 142
Lasswell, Harold D. p. 3, p. 85, 301, p. 124
Legault, Albert 247
Leiss, Amelia C. 278
LeMelle, Tilden J. 118
Lenin, V.I. 302-3, p. 124
Lepawsky, Albert 99
Lerche, Charles O., Jr. 35, p. 124
Levin, M. Gordon, Jr. 143
Levine, Robert A. 248
Lichtheim, George 304
Lieber, Robert J. 36
Lindberg, Leon N. 349-50, p. 124
Lindsey, George 247
Linklater, Andrew 86
Liska, George p. 103, 351-52, p. 124
Lorenz, Konrad 305, p. 124
Lovell, John P. 144

M

McClelland, Charles A. 37, p. 124
McGowan, Patrick J. 145-46, p. 124
MccGwire, Michael 249
McKean, Roland N. 233, p. 122
Mackinder, Sir Halford J. 192, p. 124
McLellan, David S. 38
McNamara, Robert L. 245
McNeil, Elton B. 306
Macomber, William 147
Mahan, Alfred Thayer 193, p. 124
Manning, C.A.W. 100
Mao Tse-tung 250, p. 124
Martin, Laurence W. 101
Mates, Leo 102
May, Rollo 307
Meadows, Davis L. 103
Meadows, Donella H. 103-4
Meisel, James H. 308
Mendlovitz, Saul H. 105, 336
Merritt, Richard L. 39
Midlarsky, Manus I. 309

Author Index

Miller, Neal E. p. 85
Mitrany, David p. 101, 353, p. 124
Modelski, George 148
Moon, Parker Thomas 310
Moos, Malcolm 126, p. 120
Morgan, Roger 40
Morgenstern, Oskar 194, 251, p. 125
Morgenthau, Hans J. pp. 3-4, 41, 106, 149-52, p. 57, 195, p. 125
Mueller, John E. 42
Mukerjee, Tapan 279

N

Nagel, Jack 196
Naroll, Raoul 252
Needler, Martin C. 153
Nef, John V. 253
Neustadt, Richard E. 354, p. 125
Nicolson, Harold p. 42, 154, p. 125
Niebuhr, Reinhold 107, 155, p. 125
North, Robert C. 118, 281, p. 120
Northedge, F.S. 311
Nye, Joseph S., Jr. 348, 355-56, p. 125

O

Odell, Peter R. 108
Ogburn, William Fielding 109
Olau, Arne 168
O'Leary, Michael K. 156
Organski, A.F.K. 157, 197
Organski, Katherine 197
Osgood, Robert E. 135, 158, 254, 357, p. 125

P

Paige, Glenn D. 159, p. 125
Palmer, Norman D. 110
Paxton, John 43
Pentland, Charles 358
Perkins, Howard C. 110
Pfaltzgraff, Robert L., Jr. 13, 111, 242, 255, p. 121, p. 123, p. 125
Platig, E. Raymond 44
Porter, Brian 45
Possony, Stefan T. 117

Pruitt, Dean G. 46, p. 125
Puchala, Donald James 47
Pye, Lucian W. 48

Q

Quester, George 256, 258

R

Rapoport, Anatol 49, 257
Renouvin, Pierre 50
Richardson, Lewis F. p. 3, p. 87, 312-13
Rhinelander, John B. 271
Riker, William H. p. 103, 359, p. 125
Robbins, Lionel 314
Rokkan, Stein 39
Rosecrance, Richard N. 51, p. 28, 112, 258
Rosenau, James N. p. 6, pp. 7-8, 32, 52-54, p. 41, 160-64, 315, p. 123, pp. 125-26
Rourke, Francis E. 165
Rummel, R.J. 166, p. 126
Russell, Frank Marion 55
Russett, Bruce M. 56, 113, 316-17, 360, p. 126

S

Said, Abdul A. 35, 57, p. 124
Satow, Ernest 167
Sattler, Martin J. 118
Scheingold, Stuart A. 350, p. 124
Schelling, Thomas C. 245, 259-60, p. 126
Schou, August 168
Schuman, Frederick L. 198
Schwartz, Judah L. 3
Schwarzenberger, Georg 114
Scott, Andrew M. 58
Scott, Harriet Fast 243, 263, p. 126
Scott, John Paul 318
Shepherd, George W., Jr. 118
Shubik, Martin 59, p. 126
Sills, David L. 60
Simonds, Frank H. 319
Singer, J. David p. 6, p. 7, 61, p. 28, 261, 320-21, p. 126

Author Index

Singer, Marshall R. 199
Skolnikoff, Eugene B. 118
Small, Melvin 321
Smith, Asa P. 15
Smith, Clagett C. 322
Smoke, Richard 225, p. 121
Snyder, Glenn H. 262
Snyder, Richard C. 169, p. 126
Snyder, Richard D. 46, p. 125
Sokolovskiy, V.D. 263, p. 126
Spiegel, Steven L. 120, 323, 329
Sprout, Harold 115, 200, 264, p. 126
Sprout, Margaret 115, 200, 264–65, p. 126
Spykman, Nicholas J. p. 3, 201–2, p. 126
Stanger, Roland J. 266
Stegenga, James A. 74
Steinbruner, John D. 62
Stoessinger, John G. 324
Strausz-Hupé, Robert p. 3, 116–17, 203–4, 267, p. 127
Sullivan, David S. 118

T

Tanter, Raymond 63, p. 127
Taylor, Paul 341
Thayer, Charles W. 170
Thompson, Kenneth W. 64, p. 127
Toma, Peter A. 65–66
Toscano, James V. 347
Tucker, Robert W. 254

U

Ullman, Richard H. 63, p. 127

V

Van Cleave, William R. p. 68
Van Dyke, Vernon 119
Verba, Sidney 33
Vincent, R.J. 268
Vital, David 171
Von Clausewitz, Carl 269, p. 127

W

Waltz, Kenneth N. p. 28, 323–25, p. 127
Webster, Charles 172
Weigert, Hans W. 205
Wilkenfeld, Jonathan 326, p. 127
Wilkinson, David O. 173
Wilkinson, Paul 270
Willrich, Mason 271
Winslow, E.M. 206
Wirsing, Robert G. 174
Wohlstetter, Albert p. 68, 245
Wolfers, Arnold 67, p. 127
Wright, Quincy p. 3, 68, 327, p. 127

Y

Young, Oran R. 69, 272

Z

Zawodny, J.K. 70–71, 245, p. 127
Zimmerman, William 137

TITLE INDEX

This index is alphabetized letter by letter. References are to entry numbers unless preceded by a "p." (to indicate reference is to a page number). In some cases titles have been shortened.

A

Action and Reaction in World Politics p. 28, 112
Age of Nationalism, The 96
Aggression 318
Alliance in International Politics 338, p. 121
Alliance Politics 354, p. 125
Alliances and American Foreign Policy 357
American Diplomacy, 1900-1950 140, p. 123
American Foreign Policy 141, p. 123
American Study of International Relations, The 20, p. 121
America's Role in World Politics p. 3
America's Strategy in World Politics 201, p. 126
Analysis of International Politics, The 54
Analysis of International Relations, The 12, p. 120
Analyzing International Relations 11, p. 120
Angels' Game, The 147
Approaches to Comparative and International Politics 16
Approaches to Measurement in International Relations 42
Arms and Influence 259
Arms and Insecurity p. 3, p. 87, 312
Arms Debate, The 248
Art and Practice of Diplomacy, The 172
Art of Diplomacy, The 121

B

Balance of Power and Nuclear Deterrence, The 224
Balance of Terror, The p. 68, 223, p. 121
Balance of Tomorrow, The 203
Bases of International Order, The 92
Basic Issues in International Relations 66
Between Two Ages 177, p. 120
Beyond the Nation-State p. 102, 342, p. 122
Bureaucracy and Foreign Policy 165
Bureaucratic Politics and Foreign Policy 131, p. 122

C

Causes of War, The 277
Century of Total War, The 208
Change and the Future International System 118
Changing Patterns of Military Politics 235

Title Index

Civilization and Climate p. 3, 90
Collective Security 188
Commonwealth of Man, The 198
Comparative Foreign Relations 173
Comparing Foreign Policies 162, p. 125
Comparing Nations 39
Components of Defense Policy 212
Computers and the Policy-Making Community 3
Concepts of International Politics 35, p. 124
Conflict and Defense 213, p. 119
Conflict Behavior and Linkage Politics 326, p. 127
Conflict in World Politics 323
Conflict Resolution 322
Contemporary Military Strategy 228
Contemporary Theory in International Relations 29, p. 122
Contending Approaches to International Politics p. 6, p. 7, 32, p. 123
Contending Theories of International Relations 13, p. 121
Continuities in the Study of Social Conflict 283
Contrasting Approaches to Strategic Arms Control 255
Controlling Small Wars 278
Control of the Arms Race, The 218, p. 120
Counterrevolution: How Revolutions Die 308
Crises in Foreign Policy 134, p. 122
Crisis, Escalation, War 295, p. 122
Cybernetic Theory of Decision, The 62

D

Deadly Logic 227
Decision-Making for Defense 232
Decline of Democratic Politics, The 41
Defense Strategies for the Seventies 229
Democratic Ideals and Reality 192, p. 124
Descriptive Analysis of Power, The 196

Deterrence and Defense 262
Deterrence and Strategy 210, p. 119
Deterrence, Arms Control, and Disarmament 261
Deterrence in American Foreign Policy 225, p. 121
Dimensions of Diplomacy, The 138
Dimensions of Nations 166, p. 126
Diplomacy p. 42, 154, p. 125
Diplomacy of the Great Powers, The 133
Diplomat 170
Diplomat: The World of International Diplomacy 124
Discord and Collaboration 67, p. 127
Dissolution of Power, The 176
Domestic Sources of Foreign Policy 163, p. 125
Dynamics of the Nuclear Balance, The 247

E

Ecological Perspective on Human Affairs with Special Reference to International Politics, The 200, p. 126
Economic Causes of War, The 314
Economic Consequences of the Peace, The 299, p. 123
Economic Imperialism 279
Economics of Defense in the Nuclear Age, The 233, p. 122
Economic Theories of International Politics 316, p. 126
End of the Postwar Era, The 78
Enemies in Politics 289
Essays on Intervention 266
Essence of Decision 120, p. 119
Europe: An Emergent Nation? 339, p. 121
Europe Ascendant 351
Europe's Classical Balance of Power 189, p. 121

F

Field of Nations, The 19
Footsteps into the Future 98
Force, Order and Justice 254

Title Index

Foreign Policy Decision-Making 169, p. 126
Foreign Policy in Perspective 144
From Crossbow to H-Bomb 216
From Empire to Nation 82, p. 121
Frustration and Aggression p. 85
Functioning of the International Political System, The 58
Functions of Social Conflict, The 284, p. 120
Future of Collective Violence, The 276
Future of Technological Civilization, The 187
Future of the International Stategic System, The 258

G

Game Theory and Related Approaches to Social Behavior 59, p. 126
Generals and Geographers 205
Geography and Politics in a World Divided 180
Geography and World Power 186
Geography of the Peace, The 202
Geopolitics: The Struggle for Space and Power p. 3, 204, p. 127
Global Community, The 74
Grand Strategy 219
Great Illusion, The 207
Great Powers in World Politics, The 319
Guide to Diplomatic Practice, A 167
Guide to the Study of International Relations 70

H

How Nations Negotiate 136, p. 122
Human Behavior and International Politics 320
Human Dimension in International Relations, The 300, p. 123

I

Ideals and Self-Interest in America's Foreign Relations 158, p. 125
Idea of Colonialism, The 116

Idea of National Interest, The 122, p. 119
Idea of Nationalism, The p. 3, 97, p. 123
Images of War, 1816-1965, The 321
Impasse of American Foreign Policy, The 149
Imperialism 304
Imperialism: A Study 294, p. 122
Imperialism: Highest Stage of Capitalism, The 302, p. 124
Imperialism and World Politics 310
In Defense of National Interest p. 4, 150, p. 125
Influence of Sea Power upon History, The 193, p. 124
Integration of Political Communities 347
Intermediaries, The 69
Internal War 288, p. 121
International Aspects of Civil Strife 315
International Behavior 298
International Community 331
International Conflict and Behavioral Science 291
International Conflict for Beginners 290
International Crises 26
International Disputes 311
International Encyclopedia of the Social Sciences 60
International Events and the Comparative Analysis of Foreign Policy 139, p. 123
International Organization: Politics and Process 340
International Political Communication 127
International Political Communities 333
International Politics 119
International Politics: A Framework for Analysis 89
International Politics: 1919-69 45
International Politics and Foreign Policy 53, p. 126
International Politics and the Atomic Age 88

Title Index

International Politics of Regions, The 329, p. 120
International Politics Today 47
International Regionalism 355
International Regions and the International System 360
International Relations 4
International Relations: A General Theory 5
International Relations: New Approaches 2
International Relations: Peace or War? 51
International Relations: The World Community in Transition 110
International Relations and the Future of Ocean Space 174
International Relations in the Age of Conflict between Democracy and Dictatorship 117
International Relations on the Planet Earth 17
International Relations Research 44
International Security Systems 226
International Stability 87
International Studies and the Social Sciences 52
International System: Theoretical Essays, The 33
International Systems 23
International Theory and European Integration 358
Introduction to International Politics 9
Introduction to the History of International Relations 50
Inventing the Future 85
Irony of American History, The 155

K

Korean Decision, The 159, p. 125

L

Limited War in the Nuclear Age 230
Limits to Growth, The 104
Linkage Politics p. 41, 164, p. 126
Locational Approaches to Power and Conflict 181

Logic of Images in International Relations, The 296, p. 122
Long Term Projections of Power 194

M

Mainsprings of Civilization 91
Makers of Modern Strategy 222, p. 121
Making of Foreign Policy, The 130
Man and International Relations 71, p. 127
Man, the State, and War 325, p. 127
Military Deterrence in History 252
Military Power and Potential 246, p. 123
Modern International Negotiation 142

N

Nationalism and After 79
Nationalism and Social Communication 81
National Leadership and Foreign Policy 160
Nations and Men 14
Nations in Alliance p. 103, 352, p. 124
Nations in a Multipolar World 80
Nations in Conflict 281, p. 120
Nature of Human Conflict, The 306
Nature of International Society, The 100
Neutralism and Nonalignment 101
Neutralization and World Politics 76
New Approaches to International Relations 30, p. 122
New Dimensions of World Politics 86
New Era of Ocean Politics 135
Nonalignment: Theory and Current Policy 102
Nonintervention and International Order 268
Nuclear Revolution in Soviet Military Affairs, The 243
Nuclear War and Nuclear Peace 231
Nuclear Weapons and Foreign Policy 244, p. 123
Nuclear Weapons and the Conflict of Conscience 211

Title Index

O

Oil and World Power 108
On Aggression 305, p. 124
On Escalation 236
On Guerrilla Warfare 250, p. 124
On Power: Its Nature and the History of Its Growth 182
On Revolution, Selected Greetings 1920-1966 234
On the Creation of a Just World Order 105
On Thermonuclear War 237, p. 122
On Violence 274
On War (Aron) 209, p. 119
On War (Von Clausewitz) 269, p. 127
On War: Political Violence in the International System 309
Origins of Totalitarianism 72

P

Pattern of Imperialism, The 206
Peace and the Strategy Conflict 241
Peace and War 275
Peace and War: A Theory of International Relations 73, p. 119
Peaceful Change 287
Peace in Parts 356, p. 125
Peace, War, and Numbers 317
Political Community and the North Atlantic Area 334, p. 120
Political Dynamics of European Economic Integration, The 349
Political Handbook of the War 1975 1
Political Realism and Political Idealism 27
Political Realism and the Crisis of World Politics 64, p. 127
Political Science and Area Studies 48
Political Terrorism 270
Political Unification 335, p. 121
Politics among Nations p. 3, p. 4, p. 57, 106, p. 125
Politics and Culture in International History 77, p. 119
Politics and the International System 111, p. 125
Politics of Force, The 272
Politics of Nuclear Proliferation, The 256
Population and World Politics 190
Population and World Power 197
Power 175
Power and Community in World Politics 56
Power and Equilibrium in the 1970's 178
Power and Innocence 307
Power and International Relations 179, p. 120
Power and Money 31, p. 123
Power and the Pursuit of Peace 345
Power and Wealth 191
Power Politics: A Study of World Society 114
Power through Purpose 126, p. 120
Press and Foreign Policy, The 125
Principles of Human Geography 183
Prisoner's Dilemma 49
Problems of National Strategy 245
Professional Diplomat, The 132
Protracted Conflict 267, p. 127
Psychological Dimension of Foreign Policy, The 128
Purpose of American Politics, The 151

Q

Quantitative International Politics 61, p. 126
Quantitative Techniques in Foreign Policy Analysis and Forecasting 156
Question of Imperialism, The 282, p. 120
Question of National Defense, The 251, p. 125

R

Realities of American Foreign Policy p. 4
Regional Integration 350, p. 124
Regional Politics and World Order 336
Relations of Nations, The 25

Title Index

Restoration of American Politics, The 152
Revolutionary Change 297
Rise of American Naval Power, 1776-1918 264
Role of Theory in International Relations, The 24

S

Sage International Yearbook of Foreign Policy Studies 145-46, p. 124
Salt: Implications for Arms Control in the 1970's 242, p. 123
Salt: Problems and Prospects 239
Salt: The Moscow Agreements and Beyond 271
Scientific Man Vs. Power Politics 195
Scientific Study of Foreign Policy, The 161, p. 126
Search for World Order, The 99
Shaping of Foreign Policy, The 137
Simulation in International Relations 22, p. 121
Simulation in the Study of Politics 10
Small States in International Relations 168
Social Processes in International Relations 34
Soviet Military Strategy 263, p. 126
Soviet Naval Policy 249
State and Revolution 303, p. 124
Statecraft of Machiavelli, The 123
State in International Relations, The 332
State of War, The 28, p. 122
Statesman's Year-Book, 1974-1975, The 43
Statistics of Deadly Quarrels p. 3, 313
Strategic Mobility 217
Strategy and Conscience 257
Strategy for Revolution 220
Strategy in the Missile Age 214, p. 119
Strategy of Conflict, The 260, p. 126
Strategy of Raw Materials, The 185
Structure of Nations and Empires, The 107, p. 125

Study of Future Worlds, A 83, p. 121
Study of International Affairs, The 40
Study of International Relations, The 68, p. 127
Study of War, A p. 3, 327, p. 127
Summit Conferences 1919-1960, The 129
Superpowers in a Multinuclear World, The 240, p. 123
Survival of Small States, The 171
System and Process in International Relations p. 27, 94, p. 122
Systems, States, Diplomacy and Rules 6

T

Tangle of Hopes 343
Technology and International Relations 109
Tensions That Cause Wars 280
Territorial Imperative, The 273, p. 119
Theoretical Aspects of International Relations 21
Theories of International Relations 55
Theory and Policy in International Relations 63, p. 127
Theory and Practice of International Relations, The 38
Theory and Practice in International Relations 341
Theory and Reality in International Relations 15
Theory and Research on the Causes of War 46, p. 125
Theory and the International System 37, p. 124
Theory and World Politics 36
Theory of Conflict, A 285, p. 120
Theory of Foreign Policy, A 148
Theory of International Relations: Selected Texts from Gentile to Treitschke, The 18
Theory of International Relations: The Crisis of Relevance 57
Theory of Political Coalitions, The p. 103, 359, p. 125
Theory of Political Integration, A 328
Things to Come 93

Title Index

Thinking about the Unthinkable 238
Thucydides and the Politics of Bipolarity 84
Toward a New Order of Sea Power 265
Toward a Politics of the Planet Earth 115
Toward Global Equilibrium 103
Toward the Year 2000 75
Transnational Relations and World Politics 348
Twenty Years' Crisis 1919-1939, The p. 2, 8, p. 57, p. 120

U

Understanding Foreign Policy 153
Understanding World Politics 65
Uniting of Europe, The 344, p. 122
Unity and Disintegration in International Alliances 346

W

War: The Anthropology of Armed Conflict and Aggression 292
War and Human Progress 253
War and Politics 215, p. 119
War and the Soviet Union 221
Weak States in a World of Powers 199
When Men Revolt--and Why 286
Why Federations Fail 337
Why Men Rebel 293, p. 121
Why Nations Go to War 324
Woodrow Wilson and World Politics 143
Working Peace System, A p. 101, 353, p. 124
World Communication: Threat or Promise 330
World Handbook of Political and Social Indicators 113, p. 126
World of General Haushofer, The 184
World Politics 157
World Politics and Personal Insecurity p. 3, p. 85, 301, p. 124
World Restored, A pp. 4-5, 95, p. 123
World Society 7

SUBJECT INDEX

This index is alphabetized letter by letter. If entries are preceded by a "p." they refer to page numbers. In all other cases, references are to entry numbers. Underlined numbers refer to main entries.

A

Adjudication, international. See Arbitration and mediation, international
Africa, economic integration in 333. See also Pan-Africanism
Aggressiveness 273, 292, 300, 305-6, 318
Agriculture, political integration and 339
Air warfare and defense 214, 222, 247
Alienation, political p. 86
Alliances 9, 12-13, 17, 38, 56, 61, 84, 95, 152, 168, 208, 210, 223, 226, 245, 262, 281, 309, 316, p. 103, 338, 343, 346, 352, 354, 357, 359. See also Neutrality
Allies 248
Anarchy 325
Anthropo-geography. See Geography, human
Antiballistic missiles. See Missiles and missile defense
Anti-Semitism 72
Anxiety 276
Arab-Israeli relations 141, 290, 324
Arab League 356
Arbitration and mediation, international 4, 69, 287, 311. See also Bargaining theory in international relations; Commissions of inquiry, international; Negotiations, international
Arms race p. 86, 312. See also Disarmament; Missiles and missile defense; Nuclear weapons and warfare; Strategic Arms Limitation Talks; Weapons systems
Atlantic Alliance 255
Atomic weapons. See Nuclear weapons

B

Balance of payments 31
Balance of power pp. 4-5, 13-14, 18, 25, 30, 55, 64, 67, 78, 84, 92, 94, 106, 119, 157, p. 58, 175, 178-79, 188-89, 201, 224, 226, p. 87, 301
Ballistic missiles. See Missiles and missile defense
Bargaining theory in international relations 9, 13, 30, 33, 42, 58-59, 156, 238, 259-60, 272, 317, 354. See also Game theory in in-

Subject Index

ternational relations; Negotiations, international
Bay of Pigs invasion (1961) 278
Behavioralist school of international relations pp. 5-8, 7, 19, 23, 26, 30, 32, 111, 161, 325
Bentham, Jeremy 345
Berlin Blockade (1948-49) 225, 272
Biological warfare 75
Biology and civilization 91, 318
Bipolarity in international relations pp. 27-28, 73, 80, 88, 94, 178, 226, 338, 352. See also Multipolarity in international relations
Bombers. See Air warfare and defense
Boundaries 181
Bureaucracy
  conflict within 323
  foreign policy determination and 159, 165
  in politics 63
  See also Public officials

C

Capability analysis in international relations 38, 53
Capital, politics of 31
Capitalism 304
Castroism 220, 289. See also Bay of Pigs invasion (1961); Cuban missile crisis (1962)
China
  defense and military policies of 212, 240
  history 89
  Strategic Arms Limitation Talks and 242, 255, 271
Church work. See Institutional church
Civil defense 212, 238
Civil disobedience 182. See also Revolution
Civilization, factors affecting 90-91, 186
Civil rights. See Human rights in international relations

Class conflict. See Social conflict
Clausewitz, Karl von 222, 243
Climate and civilization 90-91, 186
Club of Rome 104
Coalitions. See Alliances
Cold war 57, 124, 153, 208
Collective security 14, 64, 67, 88, 107, 157, 179, 188, 226, p. 85. See also National security
Colonialism 64, 82, 102, 116-17, 157, 281. See also Imperialism
COMECON 355
Commerce 86, 207, 343
  patterns of 360
  politics and 31
  war and 281
  See also Mercantilism
Commissions of inquiry, international 287
Common Market. See European Economic Community
Communications theory in international relations 5, 19, 34, 36-37, 56-58, 81, 124, 127, 130, 159, 163, 183, 199, 272, 295, 320, 330, 347, 360. See also Press
Communism 303, 332
  as a technique for conflict 267, 302
Competition, international 17, 101, 195, 260. See also Cooperation, international
Computers. See Game theory in international relations; Simulation and modelmaking in international relations
Concert of Europe 345
Conciliation, international. See Arbitration and mediation, international
Confederations of states 18, 94, 198, 333, 337. See also Global interdependence; Integration theory in international relations

Subject Index

Conferences, international 287.
See also Summit conferences
Conflict, international 2, 6-7, 11-13, 25, 29, 34-36, 38, 51, 54, 56, 61, 63, 66, 71, pp. 27-28, 74, 88-89, 106, 110-11, 142, 153, 162, 166, 176, 181, 195-96, pp. 68-69, 211, 213, 217-18, 221, 229, 236, 260, 266-68, pp. 85-88, 273-327, 341, 346. See also Arbitration and mediation, international; Civil disobedience; Deterrence theory; Guerrilla warfare; Revolution; Terrorism; Violence, political; War
Congress of Vienna 95
Conservation. See Ecology; Natural resources; Ocean resources
Cooperation, international 40.
See also Competition, international; Detente; Global interdependence
Corporations
foreign policy determination and 160
national behavior and 316
See also Industry; Multinational corporations; Trade associations
Counterinsurgency 212. See also Insurgency; Terrorism
Cuban missile crisis (1962) 120, 134, 225, 272, 295
Culture
civilization and 91
integration of 105
Currency 43. See also Monetary policy
Cybernetics in international relations 36, 47, 62
Czechoslovakia, foreign policy of 171

D

Decision-making in international relations 2, 5-7, 10, 13-14, 17, 23, 29-30, 38, 50, 53, 58, 62, p. 41, 127-28, 130-31, 134, 159, 169, 216, 227, 262, 295, 306, 316, 349, 356
Defense policies. See Military policies and forces; National defense; U.S. Department of Defense
Democracy 332
decline of 152
diplomacy and 154
foreign policy and 41, 153
nationalism and 82
World War II and 195
Demography in international relations 50, 204. See also Climate and civilization; Geography, human; Population
Detente 346
Deterrence theory 12, 14, 23, 42, 56, 58, 88, 142, 152, pp. 67-69, 210, 212, 214-15, 219, 221, 223-25, 227-29, 231, 233, 238, 244, 247, 252, 257-58, 261-62. See also Conflict, international; Counterinsurgency
Diplomacy 6, 14, 17, 25, 38, 63-64, 80, 106, 110, 119, pp. 42-43, 121, 124, 129, 133, 138, 140, 147, 152, 154, 157, 167, 170, 172, 259, 275
bargaining in 89
evolution and changes of 45, 51, 209
morality and 67
role and limits of 12, 73, 95, 150, 251
security and 226
of the United Nations 41, 124
See also Foreign policy; Negotiations, international; Summit conferences; U.S. Foreign Service
Diplomatic and consular service 167, 169

Subject Index

Diplomatic privileges and immunity 167, 170
Disarmament 13, 25, 47, 55, 80, 87, 106, 111, 119, 152, p. 69, 211-12, 218, 228-29, 231, 238-39, 241, 245, 247, 257, 261, 317, 343. See also Arms race; Strategic Arms Limitation Talks; Weapons systems
Dulles, John Foster 289
Dunn, Sherwood 20
Durkheim, Emile 283

E

Ecology, as a behavior determinant 83, 115, 187, 200. See also Environmental factors
Economic development 17, 343, 360
  in comparative foreign policy study 166
  conflict and 309
  models of 103
  population and 190
  role of petroleum industry in 108
  sociopolitical characteristics of 102
Economic policy 184
Economics
  in alliance theory 338
  conflict and 219, 222, 287-88, 314, 319, 323
  inequality in 99
  political 13, 31, 45, 50-51, 73, 89, 119, 175, 178, 191, 199, 206-7, 279
  statistics 1, 43
  See also International economic relations
Education
  higher 75
  as a means of avoiding conflict 195
  statistics 43
Educators
  foreign policy determination and 160
  political integration and 339

EEC. See European Economic Community
Elections, analysis of foreign 156. See also Voting behavior
Energy resources. See Natural resources; Petroleum industry
England. See Great Britain
Environmental factors
  civilization and 91
  in foreign policy determination 130, 137
  international relations and 17, 56, 112, 115, 200
  See also Ecology
Environmentalist school in international behavior 200
Equality and inequality 98
Equilibrium theory 29
Escalation. See Conflict, international
Ethics. See Political ethics
Ethnic nationalism. See Race and international relations
Europe
  history 112
  integration and cooperation in 40, 141, p. 102, 339, 351-52, 358
  Strategic Arms Limitation Talks and 255, 271
European Coal and Steel Community 344
European Economic Community 335, 349, 355
Expansionism. See Imperialism
Extra-territoriality 167

F

Factor analysis, in foreign policy research 166, 360
Fascism 332. See also Nazis; Totalitarianism
Federalist approach to political integration 355, 358
Federal-state relations 75
Field theory in international relations 53, 68, 99, 326
Finland, foreign policy of 171
Foodstuffs, as a function of power 185

Subject Index

Force. See Power (social sciences)
Foreign aid 343
  politics of 31
Foreign investment. See Investment, foreign
Foreign policy 11-12, 14, 35, 74, 78, 89, 110, 117, pp. 41-42, 120-74, 191, 290, 319
  comparative 9, 16, 137, 139, 145-46, 161, 166, 169, 173, 320
  conflict and 326
  by country
    Germany 149
    Greece 84
    Italy 123
    Russia 120, 126, 141, 149, 267
    underdeveloped countries 16, 149
    U.S. 28, 57, 65, 78, 80, 120, 122, 126, 140-41, 143-44, 149-53, 158-60, 165, 174, 190, 201-3, 205, 225, 244, 357
  decision-making in 38, 62
  democratic process and 41
  idealism and realism in 27
  Lockean theory and 15
  of major powers 25
  objectives of p. 5, 66-67, 115
  press and 125, 131
  psychological aspects of 128
  public opinion and 47
  See also Colonialism; Conflict, international; Diplomacy; Internationalism; International relations; Isolationism; Neutrality; Summit conferences
France, civil and military power in 235
Free-will environmentalist school in international behavior 200
Functionalist school of international relations pp. 101-2, 341-42, 344, 350, 353, 355-56, 358
Futurology 75, 83, 93, 105. See also Technological forecasting

G

Game theory in international relations 9, 13, 19, 30, 33, 36, 49, 53, 59, 213, 227, 238, 257, 260, 306. See also Bargaining theory in international relations; Simulation and model-making in international relations; War games
Geography, human 183. See also Demography in international relations
Geography, political 1, 43, 50, 73, 115, 157, 180-81, 184, 186, 192, 200, 202, 204-5
Germany, foreign policy of 149. See also Berlin Blockade (1948-49); Nazis
Global interdependence 17, 51, 63, 78-79, 83, 86, 92, 96, 98, 104, 106, 115, 176, 179, 360. See also Confederations of states; Cooperation, international; Integration theory in international relations; Regionalism
Governmental statistics 43
Government officials. See Bureaucracy; Public officials; Statesmen
Great Britain
  rule of India 279
  as a sea power 193
Greece
  history 84
  insurgent movements in 278
Gross national product 360
Guerrilla warfare 12, 250. See also Insurgency; Revolution; Terrorism

H

Haushofer, Karl 184, 204-5
Heredity. See Biology and civilization
Hijacking 285

Subject Index

Hilferding, Rudolf 304
History 1
   in the context of modern international relations p. 28, 77
   of Europe 112
   of Greece 84
Hobson, John A. 206, 302, 304
Human geography. See Geography, human
Human rights in international relations 40, 99
Hungarian revolution (1956) 225

I

Idealist school of international relations 27, 65, 126
Ideology 14, 21, 35, 45, 58, 65, p. 29, 72, 118, 268
Immunity. See Diplomatic privileges and immunity
Imperialism 4, 55, 72, 84, 106-7, 111, 117, 143, p. 86, 282, 294, 301-2, 304, 310
   economics of 13, 31, 206-7, 279, 314
   See also Colonialism
India
   British rule of 279
   nuclear program of 240
   relations with Pakistan 324
Indonesian War of Independence 278
Industrialization
   as a function of power 203
   warfare and 253
   See also Science; Technology
Industry, political integration and 339. See also Corporations; Multinational corporations; Trade associations
Inequality. See Equality and inequality
Information, in foreign policy determination 130. See also Communications theory in international relations
Institutional church 75
Insurgency 245. See also Counterinsurgency; Guerrilla warfare; Terrorism

Integration theory in international relations 11-13, 36, 40, 47, 53, 56, 61, 71, 87, 111, 197, pp. 87-88, pp. 101-4, 328-60. See also Cooperation, international; Detente; Global interdependence; Regionalism
Intelligence gathering 170. See also Secret police
Interdependence, global. See Global interdependence
Interest groups, in foreign policy determination 130-31, 148, 163
International disputes. See Conflict, international
International economic relations 40, 79, 117, 348. See also Balance of payments; Investment, foreign
Internationalism 4, 38, 51, 201, 330. See also Isolationism; Nationalism
International Labor Organization 342
International law 11, 14, 28, 33, 38, 45, 68, 80, 92, 106, 114, 226, 327
   foundations of 8
   in war and peace 18
   See also Arbitration and mediation, international; Diplomatic privileges and immunity; Extra-territoriality; Human rights in international relations; Law; Neutrality
International organization 4-5, 11, 14, 35, 68, 80, 92, 106, 110, 118-19, 175, 301, 340-41, 343, 345, 348, 353. See also Confederations of states; Cooperation, international; Global interdependence; Integration theory in international relations
International organizations 1, 12, 38, 45, 66, p. 29, 105, 115, 117, 142, 157, 311,

Subject Index

341, 343, 353, 355, 360.
See also Voluntary organizations; names of specific organizations
International relations
  approaches to the study of 1-72, 89, 99
  changing international system and pp. 27-29, 72-119
  evolution of pp. 1-8, 40, 45
  periodicals pp. 113-18
  recommended books for small libraries pp. 119-27
  See also Alliances; Cold war; Communications in international relations; Competition, international; Conflict, international; Decision-making in international relations; Diplomacy; Foreign policy; Global interdependence; Integration theory in international relations; Military policies and forces; Regionalism; War
Inter-Nation Simulation Project 10, 22
Inter-University Comparative Foreign Policy Project 162
Intervention. See Conflict, international; Deterrence theory
Investment, foreign 343, 348
Isolationism 17, 126, 201. See also Internationalism; Nationalism
Israel, foreign policy of 171. See also Arab-Israeli relations
Italy, foreign policy of 123

J

Japan
  foreign policy in Asia 143
  nuclear options of 240
  relationship with the U.S. 255
  Strategic Arms Limitation Talks and 271

K

Kant, Immanuel 345

Kautsky, Karl Johann 304
Khrushchev, Nikita 243
Korean War (1950-53) 134, 159, 169, 225, 230, 324

L

Labor unions. See Trade unions
Land forces 180, 192, 204, 217, 243
Latin America
  military spending in 156
  revolution in 220
Latin America Free Trade Association 333
Law, significance of 100. See also International law
Law of the Sea Conference 174
Leadership in international relations 50, 160, 162, 173
League of Nations 55, 114, p. 85, 310, 319, 345
Learning theory in international relations 53, 347
Legations. See Diplomatic and consular service
Leisure, as a potential international problem 85
Lenin, Nikolai 206, 302-4
Less developed countries. See Underdeveloped countries
Level-of-analysis problem 111
Liberalism 304
  corruption of 152
Limited war. See War, limited
Literacy 360

M

Machiavelli, Niccolo di Bernardo 123
Mackinder, Sir Harold J. 205
Mahan, Alfred Thayer 264
Marx, Karl 283, 304
Marxian economic theories 206, 314
Mass media. See Communications theory in international relations; Press
Mediation, international. See Arbitration and mediation, international

Subject Index

Mercantilism 304
Middle East. See Arab-Israeli relations
Migration. See Population
Military bases 217
Military policies and forces 51, 87, 89, 111, pp. 67-69, 207-72, 295
  expenditures for 156, 233, 281
  power and 178, 191, 199
  relations with the civilian sector 212
  strategy and deployment 210, 212, 214, 217, 219-20, 222, 228-29, 231, 239-41, 244-45, 247, 250, 253, 257, 260-61, 263, 269, 271, 275, 327
  See also Air warfare and defense; Atomic weapons and warfare; Land forces; National defense; Missiles and missile defense; Sea power; Soldiers, professional; U.S. Department of Defense; Weapons systems
Mill, James 345
Minorities. See Race in international relations
Missiles and missile defense 245, 247, 354
Mobility. See Population
Model-making and simulation in international relations. See Game theory; Simulation and model-making in international relations
Monarchy 332
Monetary policy 86. See also Currency
Morality in politics. See Political ethics
Multinational corporations p. 29
  national sovereignty and 31
  political integration and 348
Multipolarity in international relations pp. 27-28, 73, 80, 94, 178, 258, 338. See also Bipolarity in international relations

N

National characteristics
  conflict and 61, 162, 300
  foreign policy participation and 145
National defense 212, 216, 219, 228, 245, 248-49, 251, 262. See also Civil defense; Military policies and forces; Missiles and missile defense; Naval policies and forces; U.S. Department of Defense
National Guard. See U.S. National Guard
National interest 7
  conflict and 314, 316
  foreign policy determination and 122, 126, 130, 135, 150-51, 153, 158, 161, 191
Nationalism 4, 14, 25, 38, 41, 45, 47, 50-51, 55, p. 29, 72, 79-82, 96-97, 106, 111, 115, 119, 176, 208, p. 86, 301, 304, 330. See also Internationalism; Race and international relations; Regionalism; Self-determination, national; State, the
National security 64, 119, 202, 210, 229, 245, 261-62, 343. See also Collective security
Nation-state. See State, the
NATO. See North Atlantic Treaty Organization
Natural resources 78, 115, 118, 157
  conservation and shortages of 85-86, 103, 190, 194, 287
  as a function of power 180, 185, 203
  location and distribution of 183, 186, 203
  statistics 43
  See also Ocean resources
Naval policies and forces 249, 265. See also Sea power

Subject Index

Nazis, war concepts of 222. See also Fascism
Negotiations, international 135-36, 141-42, 147, 260, 287, 310. See also Arbitration and mediation, international; Bargaining theory in international relations; Diplomacy
Neutrality 23, 41, 84, 101-2, 168, 248, 338. See also Alliances
Neutralization in international relations 76
Nixon Doctrine 78
Nkrumah, Kwame 289
Nonalignment. See Neutrality
Nonintervention. See Conflict, international; Deterrence theory
Nordic Union 335
Normative school in international relations. See Utopian school in international relations
Norms, transnational 115
North Atlantic Treaty Organization 62, 231, 239, 241, 245, 357
Nuclear Proliferation Treaty (1968) 256
Nuclear sharing 245
Nuclear weapons and warfare 2, 5, 88, 168, pp. 67-68, 208-11, 214-15, 221, 223-24, 229-31, 237-43, 245, 250-51, 258, 263
  ethics of 227, 254
  tactical 244
  See also Arms race; Missiles and missile defense; Weapons systems

O

OAS. See Organization of American States
Ocean resources, in international negotiations 135, 174
Oil industry. See Petroleum industry
"Open Door" policy 140
Order, national 92, 95, 107, 275

Organization of African Unity 356
Organization of American States 355-56

P

Pacifism 55
Pakistan, relations with India 324
Pan-Africanism 333
Paris Peace Conference (1919) 299
Peace and peacekeeping 28, 47, 52, 64, 87, 99, 117, 121, 168, 207, p. 85, 275, 309, 345. See also Pacifism; War
Personality, in foreign policy determination 162-63
Petroleum industry, role in international relations 108, 156
Pluralist school of international relations 358
Police. See Secret police
Political behavior, foreign policy determination and 160. See also Voting behavior
Political ethics p. 3, 45, 64, 67, 92, 123, 182. See also Nuclear weapons, ethics of
Political geography. See Geography, political
Political integration. See Integration theory in international relations
Political leaders. See Presidents; Public officials; Statesmen
Political parties
  in foreign policy determination 130, 163
  political integration and 344
Political realism. See Realist school of international relations
Political research, use of computers in 3
Political science, study and teaching 99. See also International relations
Politics, comparative 113. See also Foreign policy, comparative

Subject Index

Politics, international. See International relations
Politics, national 16, 164
  foreign policy and 28, 161
  international politics and 99, 119
Politics and economics. See Economics, political
Politics and war. See War, politics of
Population 86, 115, 118, 157, 184, 186, 190, 360
  as a cause of conflict 281, 287
  in comparative foreign policy study 166
  as a function of power 180, 197, 203
  growth of 183
  as a potential world problem 85, 103
  statistics 1, 43
Possibilist school in international behavior 200
Poverty, elimination of 83
Power (social sciences) p. 4, p. 5, 17, 21, 38, 45, 47, 51, 56, 58, 67, 80, 114, 138, 148, pp. 57-58, 175-206, 241, 248, 274
  distribution of 105
  economic foundations of 222, 314
  management of 110-11
  national 25, 157
  nature of 8, 27, 73, 115, 117, 150, 320
  origins of 182
  struggle for 106
  theories of 36-37
  See also Balance of power
Predictions. See Futurology; Technological forecasting
Presidents
  diplomacy and 121
  foreign policy determination and 131
  See also Wilson, Woodrow
Press, foreign policy determination and 125, 131. See also Communications theory in international relations
Propaganda 38, 72, 89, 124

Psychology
  in explaining conflict pp. 85-86, 280, 286, 298, 300-301, 307, 318, 320, 325
  in foreign policy decision-making 128
  See also Aggressiveness; Anxiety; Personality
Public officials, foreign policy determination and 131, 162. See also Bureaucracy; Presidents; Statesmen
Public opinion 42, 47, 50, 89, 320
  in foreign policy determination 125, 130, 145, 160
  in political integration 350

R

Race in international relations 55, 118, 287, 300, 323. See also Nationalism
Raw materials. See Natural resources; Ocean resources
Realist school of international relations p. 3, 8, 13, 27, 29, 64-65, 106, 111, p. 41, 126, 140, 157
Regionalism 13, 47, 51, 53, 329, 336, 340-41, 350, 353, 355-56, 360. See also Global interdependence; Integration theory in international relations
Religious statistics 43
Republicanism 332
Revolution 176, 182, 219-20, 228, 234, p. 86, 285-86, 288, 297, 301, 308, 322. See also Civil disobedience; Conflict, international; Guerrilla warfare; Terrorism, Violence, political; War
Rousseau, Henri Jean Jacques 345
Russia
  defense and military policies of 212, 221-22, 239-43, 249, 255, 263, 271
  diplomatic and foreign policies of 120, 126, 141, 149,

Subject Index

267-68, 279
military concepts of 221-22
relations with the U.S. 296
See also Soviet-Iranian conflict

S

SALT. See Strategic Arms Limitation Talks
Schumpeter, Joseph 304
Science
impact on society 187
international relations and 57, 177
political integration and 343, 348
war and 219, 222
See also Industrialization; Technology
Sea bed. See Ocean resources
Sea power 180, 192-93, 204, 217, 222. See also Naval policies and forces
Secret police 72
Security. See Collective security; National security
Self-determination, national 4, 82, 303. See also Sovereignty
Separation of powers 41
Simulation and model-making in international relations 3, 5, 7, 10-11, 17, 19, 22, 30, 33-34, 42, 57, p. 27, 94, 103, 134, 137, 145, 162, 194, 281, 317, p. 103, 338, 359. See also Game theory
Smith, Adam 206
Social change 322
in international society 92
national aggressiveness and 61
Social conflict 303, 322. See also Conflict, international
"Social cosmos" 100
Social development 343
sociopolitical characteristics of 102
Social groups, conflict and 284
Socialization, international 23, 34
Social science theory
in explaining conflict 293, 298,

318, 320, 323, 325
in explaining nationalism 81
in research on international relations 44, 47, 156
See also Aggressiveness; Alienation, political; Anxiety; Psychology
Society, influence on foreign policy 160, 162-63
Soldiers, professional 34
South America. See Latin America
Sovereignty 15, 25
concepts and theories of 97, 182
multinational corporations and 31
world disorder and 198
See also Self-determination, national; State, the
Soviet-Iranian conflict 278
Spanish America. See Latin America
State, the 6, 15, 18, 35, 71-72, 82, 99-100, 107, 114, 198, 291, 332. See also Confederations of states; Nationalism; Sovereignty
States, new 5, 92, 102
democracy and 82
nonalignment of 101
States, small 146, 168, 171
Statesmen 1, 21, 38, 66, 272. See also Leadership; Public officials
Strategic Arms Limitation Talks 141, 239, 242, 247, 255, 271
Strategic theory in international relations 53
Strategy. See Military policies and forces
Suez crisis (1956) 354
Summit conferences 129. See also Conferences, international
System analysis
in conflict assessment 306, 320
in defense decision-making 216
in deterrence theory 227
in international relations 29-30, 36-37, 53, 58, 99

T

Taiwan Strait crisis (1958) 225, 272

Subject Index

Technological forecasting 75, 93, 194. See also Futurology
Technology
  arms control and 239, 242
  as a function of power 176-77, 194, 203, 241
  impact on society 187
  international relations and 45, 57, 104, 109, 111, 115, 118, p. 101
  the modern state system and 88
  political integration and 343
  war and 208, 216, 219, 222, 243, 251, 253, 268, 277, 281, 327
  See also Industrialization; Science
Territorial behavior 273
Territory, national 181. See also Boundaries
Terrorism 28, p. 29, 111, p. 69, 270, 285, 288. See also Counterinsurgency; Guerrilla warfare; Insurgency; Revolution; Violence, political; War
Threats. See Power (social sciences)
Tools, historical development of 183
Totalitarianism 72, 182. See also Fascism
Trade. See Commerce
Trade associations, political integration and 339, 344
Trade unions
  foreign policy determination and 160
  political integration and 339, 344, 348
Traditionalist school of international relations pp. 5-7, 32, 111
Transportation, growth of 183
Treaties 167. See also Alliances; Versailles, Treaty of (1919)

U

Underdeveloped countries
  change in 87
  foreign policy in 16, 149
  national-international linkages in 164

Union of Soviet Socialist Republics. See Russia
United Arab Republic 335. See also Arab-Israeli relations
United Nations 41, 69, 114, 148, 152, 226, 266, 345, 355
United States
  defense and military policies of 219, 239-42, 244, 248, 255, 265, 271
  diplomatic and foreign policies of 28, 57, 78, 80, 120, 122, 126, 140-41, 143-44, 149-53, 155, 158-60, 165, 174, 190, 201-3, 205, 225, 268, 357
  policy toward international organizations 343
  relations with Russia 296
  technology in 177
U.S. Congress
  defense spending of 145
  relationship to diplomats 147
U.S. Department of Defense 232
U.S. Foreign Service 132
U.S. National Guard 235
Utopian school of international relations p. 2, p. 3, p. 8, 8, 15, p. 29, 111, p. 41, p. 85

V

Values 58, 83, 105, 130
  conflict and 301, 307, 327
  in political integration 347
Versailles, Treaty of (1919) 299
Vietnamese War 234, 296, 324
  negotiations of the 141
Violence, political 56, 75, 98, 105, 119, 156, 235, 258-59, 272, 274-76, 283, 286, 293, 307, 317. See also Conflict, international; Guerrilla warfare; Revolution; Terrorism; War
Voluntary organizations, foreign policy determination and 160. See also International organizations

Subject Index

Voting behavior 340
   defense spending and 145
   in foreign policy determination 163
   in international organizations 42, 166, 360
   See also Elections

W

War 28, 34, 66, 68, 106, 119, 184, 215, 248, 292, 309, 321
   in the atomic age 211
   behavioral indicators of 146
   causes of 18, 46, 61, 73, 277, 280, 312, 317, 324-25
   diplomacy and 121
   economics of 13, 31, 314, 325
   elimination of 83
   limited 208, 214, 217, 219, 228, 230-31, 244, 278
   nature of 35, 99, 209, 263, 275, 303
   politics and 269, 274
   psychological aspects of 280, 300-301
   technology and 253, 277
   See also Air warfare and defense; Biological warfare; Conflict, international; Guerrilla warfare; Military policies and forces; Nuclear weapons and warfare; Peace and peacekeeping; Revolution; Terrorism; Violence, political; names of specific wars

War games, computer simulation in 3
Warsaw Pact (1955) 357
Washington Conference (1922) 265
Wealth
   distribution of 105
   power and 191
Weapons systems 85, 216. See also Arms race; Missiles and missiles defense; Nuclear weapons and warfare
West Indies Federation 335
White House Conference on Foreign Aid (1957) 160
Wilson, Woodrow 143
World government. See Global interdependence
World politics. See International relations
World War I p. 86, 281, 324
World War II 195, 201-2, 205, 214, p. 86, 295, 324

Y

Yugoslavia, nonalignment policies of 102